The Roman Empire

Don Nardo

LUCENT BOOKS

An imprint of Thomson Gale, a part of The Thomson Corporation

THOMSON

GALE™

Detroit • New York • San Francisco • San Diego • New Haven, Conn. • Waterville, Maine • London • Munich

© 2006 Thomson Gale, a part of The Thomson Corporation.

Thomson and Star Logo are trademarks and Gale and Lucent Books are registered trademarks used herein under license.

For more information, contact
Lucent Books
27500 Drake Rd.
Farmington Hills, MI 48331-3535
Or you can visit our Internet site at http://www.gale.com

LIBRARY OF CONGRESS CATALOGING-IN-PUBLICATION DATA

Nardo, Don, 1947–
   The Roman Empire / by Don Nardo.
      p. cm. — (The world history series)
   Includes bibliographical references and index.
    ISBN 1-59018-657-5 (hard cover : alk. paper) 1. Rome—History—Empire, 30
B.C.–476 A.D.—Juvenile literature. I. Title. II. Series.
DG270.N37 2005
937'.06—dc22
                                                    2005015850

Printed in the United States of America

Contents

Foreword

Each year, on the first day of school, nearly every history teacher faces the task of explaining why his or her students should study history. Many reasons have been given. One is that lessons exist in the past from which contemporary society can benefit and learn. Another is that exploration of the past allows us to see the origins of our customs, ideas, and institutions. Concepts such as democracy, ethnic conflict, or even things as trivial as fashion or mores, have historical roots.

Reasons such as these impress few students, however. If anything, these explanations seem remote and dull to young minds. Yet history is anything but dull. And therein lies what is perhaps the most compelling reason for studying history: History is filled with great stories. The classic themes of literature and drama—love and sacrifice, hatred and revenge, injustice and betrayal, adversity and overcoming adversity—fill the pages of history books, feeding the imagination as well as any of the great works of fiction do.

The story of the Children's Crusade, for example, is one of the most tragic in history. In 1212 Crusader fever hit Europe. A call went out from the pope that all good Christians should journey to Jerusalem to drive out the hated Muslims and return the city to Christian control. Heeding the call, thousands of children made the jour-

ney. Parents bravely allowed many children to go, and entire communities were inspired by the faith of these small Crusaders. Unfortunately, many boarded ships captained by slave traders, who enthusiastically sold the children into slavery as soon as they arrived at their destination. Thousands died from disease, exposure, and starvation on the long march across Europe to the Mediterranean Sea. Others perished at sea.

Another story, from a modern and more familiar place, offers a soul-wrenching view of personal humiliation but also the ability to rise above it. Hatsuye Egami was one of 110,000 Japanese Americans sent to internment camps during World War II. "Since yesterday we Japanese have ceased to be human beings," he wrote in his diary. "We are numbers. We are no longer Egamis, but the number 23324. A tag with that number is on every trunk, suitcase and bag. Tags, also, on our breasts." Despite such dehumanizing treatment, most internees worked hard to control their bitterness. They created workable communities inside the camps and demonstrated again and again their loyalty as Americans.

These are but two of the many stories from history that can be found in the pages of the Lucent Books World History series. All World History titles rely on sound research and verifiable evidence, and all give students a clear sense of time, place, and chronology through maps and time-lines as well as text.

All titles include a wide range of author-itative perspectives that demonstrate the complexity of historical interpretation and sharpen the reader's critical thinking skills. Formally documented quotations and annotated bibliographies enable students to locate and evaluate sources, often instantaneously via the Internet, and serve as valuable tools for further research and debate.

Finally, Lucent's World History titles present rousing good stories, featuring vivid primary source quotations drawn from unique, sometimes obscure sources such as diaries, public records, and con-temporary chronicles. In this way, the voices of participants and witnesses as well as important biographers and histo-rians bring the study of history to life. As we are caught up in the lives of others, we are reminded that we too are characters in the ongoing human saga, and we are better prepared for our own roles.

ca. 30 B.C.–A.D. 180
The approximate years of the so-called Pax Romana ("Roman Peace"), a period of relative peace and prosperity.

98–117
Reign of the emperor Trajan, during which the Roman Empire reaches its greatest extent of size and power.

27
The Roman Senate confers on Octavian the title of Augustus, and he becomes, in effect, Rome's first emperor.

14
Augustus dies, plunging the Roman people into a period of deep mourning; he is succeeded by Tiberius.

50	1	50	100	150	200

B.C. **A.D.**

25
The Han dynasty is founded in China.

224
The Sassanian Persian Empire is established in the region now occupied by Iran and Iraq.

4
Jesus Christ is born in Bethlehem (in the Roman province of Judaea).

79
The volcano Mt. Vesuvius erupts, burying the Italian towns of Pompeii and Herculaneum.

64
A great fire ravages large sections of Rome; the emperor Nero unfairly blames the disaster on the Christians.

History of the Roman Empire

330
Constantine inaugurates the city of Constantinople, located on the Bosphorus Strait.

ca. 376
The Huns sweep out of Asia and destroy the kingdom of the Ostrogoths.

451
Attila, a widely feared leader of the Huns, is defeated at Chalons, in Gaul, and the Hunnish empire quickly disintegrates.

| 250 | 300 | 350 | 400 | 450 | 500 |

284
Former soldier Diocletian ascends Rome's throne and initiates sweeping political, economic, and social reforms.

320
The Gupta Empire is founded, encompassing most of northern India.

410
The Visigoths sack the city of Rome.

313
The emperors Constantine and Licinius issue the so-called Edict of Milan, granting religious toleration to the Christians.

476
The last Western emperor, Romulus Augustulus, is driven from his throne, marking the so-called fall of Rome.

The Evidence from the Ashes

On August 24, A.D. 79, a large-scale natural disaster struck suddenly on the western coast of Italy about 120 miles (193km) south of Rome. At the time, this thriving city of at least a million people was the capital of the Roman Empire. Consisting of all the lands surrounding the Mediterranean Sea, the Empire was the largest and the strongest military and political power on Earth. But while Roman might had conquered the known world, it could not stand up to nature's unleashed fury. The towering volcano called Vesuvius, located near the Bay of Naples, awakened after thousands of years of dormancy and began spewing out enormous quantities of noxious gases, rocks, and ash.

The immediate effects of the catastrophe were most severe for the inhabitants of Pompeii and Herculaneum—two Roman towns situated only a few miles from the volcano. The Roman scholar Pliny the Elder and his nephew, Pliny the

Younger, were then staying in a house on the bay and witnessed the eruption from a distance. The younger Pliny later penned a detailed letter describing his intrepid uncle's attempt to examine the eruption's effects up close. "On Mt. Vesuvius broad sheets of fire and leaping flames blazed at several points," one riveting section of the letter begins.

> My uncle tried to allay the fears of his companions . . . [who were] in darkness, blacker and denser than any ordinary night, which they relieved by lighting torches. . . . My uncle decided to go down to the shore and investigate on the spot the possibility of any escape by sea, but he found the waves still too wild and dangerous.[1]

Although a number of people escaped the disaster, many, including the elder Pliny, died. And a thick layer of volcanic debris buried the two towns. In the years that followed, the Romans largely abandoned the site, and in time Pompeii and Herculaneum were forgotten.

But these towns were destined for a rebirth of a different sort. The Pompeians' tragedy later became the modern world's good fortune when, in the 1700s, treasure hunters and scholars began to unearth the remains of the buried cities. Luckily, the hardened ash had preserved nearly everything. As a result, visiting Pompeii today is almost like stepping into the past. It affords one an enlightening and exciting, if sometimes eerie, glimpse of the layout and atmosphere of a town of the Roman Empire at its height. "No mirror of the past could possibly be more vivid than the reflection offered us by Pompeii and Herculaneum," writes prolific classical scholar Michael Grant.

A visit to the two places is an experience that can be paralleled nowhere else in the world. In that

Mt. Vesuvius looms menacingly behind the ruins of Pompeii. The city was buried by volcanic debris in August A.D. 79.

This nineteenth-century painting depicts the great eruption that erased Pompeii from the map and killed Pliny the Elder.

strange vacuum, its emptiness underlined by innumerable signs of long-arrested activity, life and death seem to be on particularly intimate terms.[2]

Indeed, the ruins of these towns reveal many of the habits, customs, and likes and dislikes of the ancient Romans who built them. The evidence unearthed from the ashes of Pompeii, from other sites around the Mediterranean sphere, and from surviving ancient writings shows that the Romans were highly practical, industrious, and resourceful. They were also supremely confident in their own institutions and way of life. They strongly believed that they had the best and most logical system yet devised and often aggressively imposed that system on others. It is no wonder that for hundreds of years they held sway over a huge realm consisting of many and diverse lands and peoples. Until Roman civilization eventually declined and thousands of towns like Pompeii crumbled and vanished, the adage "All roads lead to Rome" was in large degree a fact. Thanks to a random act of nature, Pompeii, located on one of those ancient highways, remains to testify to the greatness of its builders.

Chapter One

From Republic to Empire: The Augustan Age

January 16, 27 B.C., was a special day for the Roman people. Large crowds gathered to witness the members of the Senate, Rome's venerable legislature, heap honors on a thin, sandy-haired young man who walked with a slight limp. Though physically unassuming, he bore an air of great intelligence and self-assurance. His name was Octavian, and all present recognized him as the most powerful man in the known world.

A solemn and elaborate ceremony followed in which the senators thanked Octavian for his military exploits, which they claimed had saved the country. They presented him with a laurel wreath, a symbol of honor and glory, and a golden shield inscribed with his new name, Augustus, "the Revered One." At the same time, he retained the family name of Caesar, handed down from his adoptive father, Julius Caesar. In Augustus's honor, the senators changed the name of the Roman month of Sextilis to August and

ordered the minting of special coins bearing his image.

A Long and Turbulent History

Although this event marked the beginning of what came to be called the Roman Empire, it was not the beginning of the Roman nation. When Augustus's reign began, Rome was already a large and powerful empire with a long and turbulent history. The use of the word *Empire* with a capital *E* later became a convenience to differentiate the new Rome, a dictatorial state ruled by Augustus and his successors, from the Rome of the past, a more democratic state known as the Republic.

The Romans were descended from primitive tribes that settled in western Italy in about 1000 B.C. They called themselves Latins and spoke a language of the same name. Initially, they established farming villages on seven hills near a bend in the Tiber River about 15 miles (24km) inland from the seacoast. Around 750 B.C. these villages combined into a town called Rome, which at the time controlled only a few dozen square miles of territory.

At first, kings ruled Rome. In 509 B.C., however, the Romans abolished the kingship and established the Republic, a government run by elected citizens. It was far from a true democracy because only free adult males, a relatively small portion of the population, were allowed to become citizens. But it was a good deal more democratic and enlightened than an absolute monarchy. A group of citizens met periodically in an assembly, where they discussed important issues and once a year elected two officials called consuls to run the government. The Senate, made up exclusively of wealthy landholders known as patricians, advised the consuls. In the beginning, well-to-do patricians totally controlled the government. But eventually the common people, called plebeians, or plebs, won the right to have their own assembly and make laws. The plebs also elected officials known as tribunes, who had the power to veto any law.

The Roman Republic proved to be both flexible and popular and was a source of pride and patriotism for the people. Practical, hardworking, and used to hardships, the Romans came to believe that their system and ways were superior and that they were destined to rule others. This attitude, revealed in their speeches and writings, was strengthened by their belief that the gods favored their nation above all others.

Supposedly with the blessing of the gods, Roman armies marched outward in the fifth century B.C. and began conquering neighboring peoples. A long series of bloody wars ensued, during which Rome took control of all of Italy. The armies then pushed outward across the Mediterranean Sea and conquered the rich trading nation of Carthage, centered in northern Africa. The large islands of Sicily, Corsica, and Sardinia, as well as most of what are now Spain and southern France, were in Roman hands by the dawn of the second century B.C. Then Rome turned eastward and conquered Greece and most of Asia Minor

This statue of Augustus shows him in an idealized pose befitting an emperor, although he never used that title.

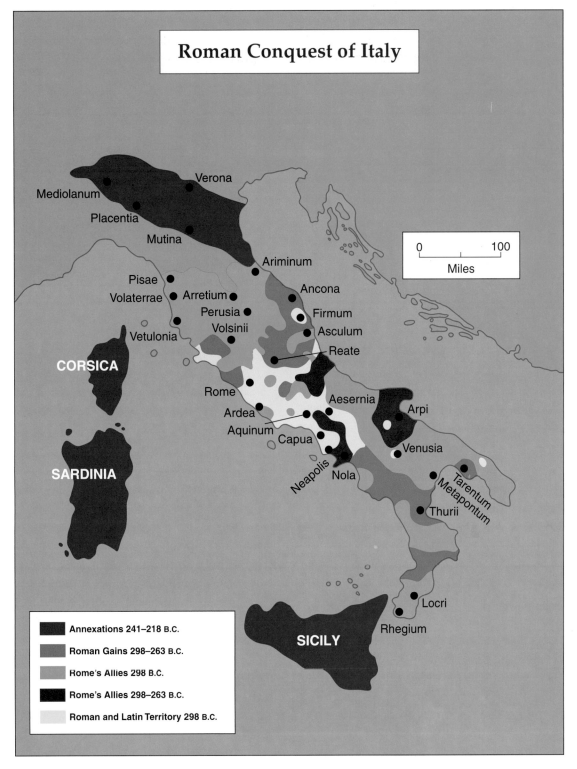

Roman Conquest of Italy

Verona
Mediolanum
Placentia
Mutina
Ariminum
Pisae
Volaterrae
Arretium
Ancona
Perusia
Firmum
Volsinii
Asculum
Vetulonia
Reate

CORSICA

Rome
Aesernia
Arpi
Ardea
Aquinum
Venusia
Capua
Neapolis
Nola
SARDINIA
Tarentum
Metapontum
Thurii

Locri
SICILY
Rhegium

0   100
Miles

Annexations 241–218 B.C.

Roman Gains 298–263 B.C.

Home's Allies 298 B.C.

Rome's Allies 298–263 B.C.

Roman and Latin Territory 298 B.C.

This nineteenth-century Italian painting depicts the members of the conspiracy against Caesar stabbing him to death in the Senate.

(what is now Turkey). By the beginning of the first century B.C. the Mediterranean had become, in essence, a Roman lake, and Rome was the most powerful nation on Earth.

The Fall of the Republic

But Rome's phenomenal success came at a price. As their realm grew, the Romans found it increasingly difficult to administer so many diverse lands and peoples. Also, conquest and rule required large, well-trained armies and skilled generals. Some generals gained great wealth and power and could be counted on to secure pensions and land for their men upon

retirement. Consequently, in time the soldiers began to show more allegiance to their generals than to the government. From the beginning of the first century B.C. onward, control of Rome's armies shifted steadily away from the Senate and the consuls to the generals. Repeated power struggles among military strongmen ignited bloody civil wars and put the Republic increasingly in jeopardy.

The most successful of these strongmen—Julius Caesar—had emerged victorious by the mid-40s B.C. He realized that Rome's republican government had become ineffective and believed that one-man rule would be more orderly and efficient. But Caesar angered many Romans when he imposed restrictions on the Senate and proclaimed himself dictator for life. On March 15, 44 B.C., a group of disgruntled senators assassinated Caesar.

The power vacuum left by Caesar's death was filled by two able generals, Mark Antony and Marcus Lepidus; and by Octavian, Caesar's eighteen-year-old adopted son. The three joined forces in 43 B.C. and used their military muscle to intimidate the government. But the alliance did not last. Another power struggle and civil war followed, eventually leaving Octavian the undisputed victor and strongest man in Rome.

Rome's Sole Master

After nearly a century of political unrest and civil wars, Rome's government was in shambles and its people frustrated and war-weary. Like Caesar, Octavian believed that Rome needed the order and stability that one able and well-meaning ruler could provide. To avoid Caesar's fate, however, Octavian wisely avoided openly declaring himself dictator. Instead, he announced his intention to restore the Republic to its former authority. "May I be privileged," he said,

> to build firm and lasting foundations for the government of the State. May I also achieve the reward to which I aspire: that of being known as the author of the best possible constitution, and of carrying with me, when I die, the hope that these foundations will abide secure.[3]

Octavian made a great show of his respect for the Senate and other republican institutions; and he encouraged the Assembly to go on electing public officials.

Augustus Subdivides the Roman Capital

To make Rome's upkeep and administration easier, Augustus subdivided the city into fourteen districts, called *regiones*. Each district further broke down into several *vici*, the counterpart of modern wards or precincts. There were more than two hundred *vici* in all. Each *vicus* had four *magistri*, local administrators who were elected annually by the people who lived in that ward. These elections were one way that Augustus maintained the fiction of the continuity of republican institutions and gave the people the feeling that they had a say in how they were governed. In reality, the *magistri* had little real authority and usually merely carried out the policies handed down from above, a chain of command stretching upward to Augustus himself. Through this administrative chain, Augustus oversaw widespread and impressive improvements in Rome's infrastructure (system of public facilities and services).

But all this was indeed show. In reality, Octavian was sole master of Rome, partly because he controlled the army. Without an army to enforce its wishes, the Senate was powerless. He also solidified his power by funding popular public programs that distributed free food to the poor. In addition, because he had already eliminated all powerful political and military opponents, he brought peace to the Roman realm. According to the first-century A.D. Roman historian Tacitus:

> He seduced the army with bonuses, and his cheap food policy was successful bait for civilians. Indeed, he attracted everybody's good will by the enjoyable gift of peace, then he gradually pushed ahead and absorbed the functions of the Senate, the officials, and even the laws.[4]

Because of his military power, his popularity, and his willingness to allow the old government the appearance that it was in charge, Octavian won the allegiance, even if halfhearted at first, of the senators. Many of them came to believe, as he did, that a benign dictator could bring order and prosperity to the country. So they obligingly granted him various titles and honors and acknowledged the wide range of governmental powers he had amassed. In addition to receiving the title of Augustus, he exercised direct control over most of the important provinces, including Egypt. He was also granted the powers of consul and tribune for life. This meant that he could make or veto any law. Although the Assembly went on electing local officials, they were almost always his approved nominees.

Augustus held so many diverse powers that he was, in fact, an emperor. To retain his popularity, however, he prudently refrained from using that title. Instead, he called himself *princeps*, meaning "first citizen." To further bolster his image as a man of the people, he and his wife, Livia, lived in a modest house and shunned the usual lavish lifestyle of the wealthy.

Peace and Prosperity

Those senators and other Romans who secretly worried that Augustus would eventually abandon this modest pose and lapse into corruption and tyranny were in for a pleasant surprise. Unlike most other dictators in history, he ruled fairly, wisely, and constructively. His peaceful and largely prosperous forty-two-year reign came to be called the Augustan Age. It turned out to be the beginning phase of a longer period of prosperity—the Pax Romana, or "Roman Peace," destined to last nearly two centuries.

Thus, Augustus kept his promise to build a lasting foundation for the country and the Empire. As the generation with firsthand memories of the Republic died out, most people looked back at it as a time of troubles and chaos. They were thankful for the peace and order Augustus had brought them.

Part of this new Augustan order consisted of a series of reforms that affected Roman institutions and customs at all levels. The military was reorganized, for example. In republican days, there had been more than thirty legions (regiments

A Monument to the Augustan Peace

Of the many buildings Augustus erected, the Ara Pacis, or "Altar of Peace," was seen by many as the crowning artistic masterpiece of his reign. Completed in January 9 B.C., it was intended as a monument to the era of peace he had initiated following the devastating civil wars. Leading magistrates and state priests and priestesses sometimes performed sacrifices beside the structure. Made of blocks of travertine, a creamy-white variety of limestone, and marble, the altar was U-shaped, with its open end facing west and accessed by a staircase. A marble wall about 30 feet square (3 sq. m) and 16 feet (5m) high enclosed the structure. On the outside of the east wall artists carved beautiful relief sculptures, including one of the goddess Roma (divine spirit of the capital city) sitting atop a pile of armor between Honos and Virtus (the spirits of honor and virtue). Also prominent was a sculpture of Pax (goddess of peace). The exteriors of the north and south walls featured horizontal bands of sculptures containing more than one hundred human figures, including Augustus himself; his wife, Livia; and his associate and son-in-law, Marcus Agrippa.

In the twentieth century, the Altar of Peace was restored using its original pieces.

of about five thousand men each) on constant active duty. For the sake of efficiency, Augustus reduced the number of legions. He also raised the soldiers' pay and introduced regular government pensions, consisting of bonuses and land, thus greatly reducing the threat of wealthy generals creating personal armies to oppose the state.

Augustus created some new military and paramilitary forces as well. One was the Praetorian Guard, a force of several thousand elite soldiers charged with guarding him and ensuring that his directives were carried out. He also recruited about three thousand policemen and some seven thousand firefighters for the city of Rome.

Sections of the outer wall and interior of the Theater of Marcellus still stand in Rome.

In addition, Augustus reformed the administration of the provinces. Under the Republic, the provincial governors had served short terms and were inexperienced, so mismanagement and corruption had been common. In the new system, more capable governors were appointed. And they were allowed to serve for several years, so that they could carry out long-term policies. Those who did well were rewarded, while those who ruled poorly were demoted.

Builder and Arts Patron

Augustus was also a prodigious builder. During his reign numerous new roads were constructed and older ones repaired. A number of harbors were built as well, facilitating and expanding trade, which flourished as never before. Augustus also built a number of aqueducts, channels that carried water from mountain streams and lakes to towns and cities.

Even more numerous were the fine public structures erected by Augustus. In 29 B.C. he completed and dedicated a new Senate house, which Julius Caesar had earlier begun, to replace one that had burned down twenty-three years before. Other imposing Augustan buildings included a temple of Apollo, god of prophecy and healing, on Rome's Palatine Hill; additions to the existing Circus Maximus, the capital's immense facility for chariot races; three temples to Jupiter, leader of the gods; and the Ara

Pacis ("Altar of Peace"), a stunning stone memorial to the peaceful era initiated by Augustus. In addition, as he boasted in his autobiography, the *Res gestae*: "On ground bought for the most part from private owners I built the theater adjoining the Temple of Apollo."[5] Completed in 11 B.C., the magnificent Theater of Marcellus sat fourteen thousand persons, making it the largest of Rome's three stone theaters.

That Augustus was proud of erecting the theater is not surprising, for he was an ardent admirer and sponsor of the arts, especially literature. Indeed, his reign later came to be seen as Rome's golden literary age. He and several of his wealthy friends patronized (provided financial and moral support for) numerous poets and prose writers. The most famous of these writers was Virgil. His long poem, the *Aeneid*, tells the legendary story of the founding of the Roman race by the Trojan prince Aeneas. The work became Rome's national patriotic epic, and every schoolboy could recite long sections of it from memory. Other outstanding writers of the Augustan Age included the poets Horace, Ovid, and Propertius, and the historian Livy.

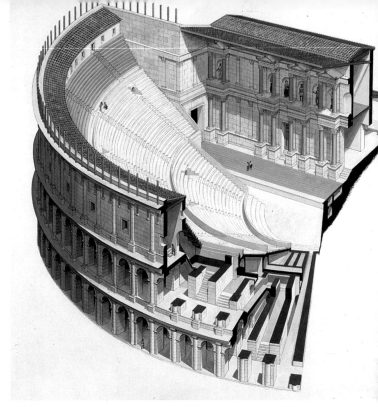

This modern restoration of the Theater of Marcellus shows its seating area, stage, and stage house (the scenae frons).

A Fitting End for a Great Ruler

In A.D. 13, at the age of seventy-six, Augustus sensed that he did not have long to live and worried about who would take his place when he died. He had no surviving male children of his own. So he decided to legally adopt and entrust the realm to Tiberius, Livia's son from a previous marriage.

That realm was enormous. It included all the lands bordering the Mediterranean as well as parts of central Europe and Gaul (what is now France)—in all, an area larger than the continental United States. Augustus urged Tiberius to make no more attempts to expand Rome's borders. Instead, the older man advised the younger to concentrate his efforts on ruling the existing realm wisely and efficiently.

After that Augustus's health steadily declined until, on August 19, in the year 14, he lay on his deathbed, surrounded by

This is how Rome's main square, the Forum Romanum, looked in Augustus's reign. Among the buildings shown are the temples of Vesta, Castor, and Saturn.

family and friends. Reportedly, he mustered the little energy he had left and uttered the words traditionally used to end Roman comedies in the theater: "Since well I have played my part, clap now your hands and with applause dismiss me from the stage." He then embraced his wife, whispered something in her ear, and quietly closed his eyes forever.

In the days that followed, millions of people across the Empire mourned the loss of the leader they had come to deeply respect and love. Many wept openly as a group of senators carried Augustus's body through the streets of the capital. An enormous crowd watched his cremation and the release of a lone eagle, whose upward flight symbolized his spirit ascending toward the gods. It was a fitting end for one of history's best and most beloved rulers, a man who had indeed played his part well.

Chapter Two

Rome of the Caesars: The First Century of Peace

The first century A.D. was a largely peaceful and prosperous era for the Roman Empire. Because Augustus had ruled so efficiently and benevolently, most desires and ambitions to bring back the Republic had died out during his long reign. All over the realm trade flourished, new towns sprang up, and living standards rose. Even many of the poor benefited, thanks to government-sponsored food distribution programs and the erection of new temples, theaters, and other public buildings. The vast majority of people were satisfied with this situation. So there was virtually no opposition to the continuation of one-man rule after Augustus's death. In accordance with his wishes, in A.D. 14 the Senate bestowed all his titles and powers on the fifty-five-year-old Tiberius.

Like Augustus, Tiberius retained the family name of Caesar. The new emperor and his three successors, all related to Augustus, formed the Empire's first dynasty (family line of rulers). Meanwhile, the name *Caesar* became an imperial title, given to all emperors regardless of heritage. Under the Augustan dynasty and the Flavian dynasty that followed, the emperors continued to operate the political and economic systems Augustus had put into place. Some of these rulers were less effective than others. But overall the Pax Romana remained in effect, and the Empire thrived.

A Capable but Unpopular Ruler

From the beginning, Tiberius recognized that, to keep the government and economy running smoothly, he had to perpetuate his stepfather's policies. So at first the new emperor allowed the Senate, the courts, and many other institutions to continue functioning normally. Like Augustus, Tiberius governed efficiently. He administered the provinces well, and the army remained disciplined and loyal under his

MVNIFICENTIA · PII · SEXTI · P · M

This woodcut shows Tiberius lounging in his villa at Capri. Back in Rome, his deputy, Sejanus, imposed a reign of terror.

rule. Moreover, he managed the economy honestly and wisely, creating a large surplus in the treasury.

Despite his abilities and good intentions, however, Tiberius eventually became unpopular with both the Senate and the people. A few Romans grumbled when he abolished the popular assemblies that had

A statue of the emperor Tiberius shows him wearing the traditional Roman toga. Though well-meaning, he became unpopular.

long elected public officials. Because these bodies now largely rubber-stamped the emperor's nominees, Tiberius reasoned that they had become meaningless and wasteful. But far more people came to resent the emperor because he spent a good deal less money staging chariot races and public games than his predecessor had.

The senators and other upper-class Romans resented Tiberius after he began delegating many of his governing duties to an ambitious and disreputable younger man, Lucius Sejanus, head of the Praetorian Guard. Sejanus, Tacitus writes, was an "audacious character" who was

> secretive about himself and ever ready to incriminate others. He concealed behind a carefully modest exterior an unbounded lust for power. Sometimes this impelled him to lavish excesses, but more often to incessant work. And that is as damaging as excess when the throne is its aim.[6]

Not surprisingly, Sejanus was delighted when, in the year 26, Tiberius decided that life would be simpler and more pleasant away from the political arena. The emperor moved his main residence to the island of Capri, about 100 miles (161km) south of Rome, and left Sejanus to run the government. It did not take long for the latter to institute a reign of terror in the capital. His spies were everywhere, and numerous senators and other prominent officials were denounced and executed for mere suspicion of wrongdoing. Eventually, Tiberius determined that Sejanus was conspiring to seize the throne and had him arrested and executed. But it was too late to undo the terrible damage the younger man had done. Tiberius died a lonely and widely hated man in 37 after a reign of twenty-three years.

Corrupted by Power?

Tiberius had no living sons, so Augustus's only living great-grandson, twenty-five-year-old Gaius Caesar, became the next emperor. Because his father had been a general, Gaius had spent much of his early childhood in army camps, where the soldiers had affectionately nicknamed him Caligula, meaning "Little Boots." Although the young man hated the name, it stuck. What also stuck to him in the eyes of history was a well-deserved reputation for extravagance, cruelty, and sexual perversion.

Caligula did not earn his bad reputation immediately, however. At first, because his youth, energy, and outgoing personality contrasted sharply with Tiberius's retiring character, the senators liked him. And because the new emperor quickly began spending large sums of money on public games, the people liked him, too. In fact, at first Caligula showed every sign that he would administer the Empire in the tradition of Augustus.

But this promise was never fulfilled. The reasons for Caligula's descent into corruption and tyranny remain uncertain. Some historians point out that he became seriously ill in 38, six months after he became emperor. According to this view, the illness may have left his mind permanently unbalanced. Other observers believe that the young man was simply corrupted by the enormous absolute power at his disposal.

Whatever the cause, Caligula's reign was a disgrace. He became convinced that his personal whims should be treated as law and bragged to his grandmother, "Bear in mind that I can treat anyone exactly as I please!"[7] The young ruler proceeded to put this arrogant belief into practice, disregarding the public good. In less than two years he spent the entire treasury surplus that Augustus and Tiberius had built up. Caligula also murdered and tortured many people. According to the first-century A.D. Roman historian Suetonius, Caligula told the consuls, "I have only to give one nod and both your throats will be cut on the spot."[8] Fortunately for Rome, Caligula's ministers and governors kept the administration of the Empire running smoothly during his short reign (37–41), which ended with his murder by his own bodyguards.

Expansion Under Claudius

The man who succeeded Caligula, his uncle Claudius, personally ensured the realm's continued prosperity by bringing back competent, effective leadership. This surprised many people because for years Claudius had appeared to be a quiet, timid man with no outstanding leadership abilities. He proved himself to be quite capable, however, and gained popularity with both the soldiers and the general populace. He built hundreds of roads, aqueducts, temples, and other public works. He also greatly expanded the civil service in the provinces, appointing many new and capable governors and other officials.

Claudius's most important achievement was the expansion of Rome's frontiers. The Empire's borders had remained about the same under his three predecessors and he felt it was time for new growth. In 43 he ordered the invasion of Britain. Julius Caesar had led troops there a century before, but the Romans, then preoccupied

Caligula lies murdered on the floor in this nineteenth-century painting. The Praetorians hail Claudius (behind the curtain) as the new emperor.

with incessant civil wars, had not followed up on the campaign. Claudius did so. Proving himself far from timid, he even traveled to Britain and toured the front lines. The campaign was ultimately successful, and the region became the province of Britannia.

Unfortunately for Claudius, he was not so accomplished in managing the affairs of his own family. His third wife, Messalina, plotted to kill him and place one of her secret lovers on the throne. In 48 Claudius discovered the plot and executed her. Next, he married Agrippina the Younger, Caligula's sister, and his own niece, another power-hungry, scheming woman. In 51 Agrippina convinced the emperor to adopt her son Nero as his son

A Compassionate Ruler

Claudius demonstrated that he was a compassionate ruler by addressing the plight of some of Roman society's underprivileged elements, foreshadowing a series of progressive social policies and laws that would be part of an emerging state welfare system in the next century. He sponsored a law that ensured that orphans would be assigned proper guardians, for instance. Here, from The Twelve Caesars, *Suetonius tells how the emperor also went out of his way to help a group of mistreated slaves.*

Finding that a number of sick or worn-out slaves had been marooned by their owners on the Island of Aesculapius, in the Tiber, to avoid the trouble of giving them proper medical attention, Claudius freed them all and ruled that none who got well again should return to the control of his former owner; furthermore, that any owner who made away with a sick slave, rather than abandon him, should be charged with murder.

A marble bust captures the features of Claudius, a largely progressive and effective ruler.

and heir. Three years later, she poisoned her husband, and Nero, then sixteen, ascended the throne.

An Infamous Reign

Nero proved to be one of the most corrupt and infamous despots in history. His ancient biographer, Suetonius, sums up the kind of man he was in this passage:

> Nero practiced every kind of obscenity, and after defiling almost every part of his body finally invented a novel game. He was released from a cage dressed in the skins of wild animals and attacked the private parts of men and women who stood bound to stakes.[9]

Nero's other violent acts included, among others, personally murdering or ordering the deaths of his stepbrother, mother, first wife (Octavia), second wife (Poppaea), and numerous Roman citizens.

Among the latter were members of a new and still small-scale religious sect—the Christians. After an enormous fire destroyed large sections of the capital in July 64, Nero accused the Christians of starting the blaze. He may have been trying to avert suspicions that he himself had initiated the fire (an accusation that was almost certainly untrue). In any case, Tacitus reports that a number of Christians "were torn to pieces by dogs, or crucified, or made into torches to be ignited after dark as substitutes for daylight."[10] This was the first of numerous government-sponsored persecutions of Roman Christians.

Viewing Nero as a despotic, dangerous individual, a number of high-placed

A nineteenth-century painting depicts the despot Nero and his courtiers gathered to watch bound Christians (at right) become human torches.

Nero Learns About Galba's Rebellion

In The Twelve Caesars, *Suetonius tells how, when news of Galba's rebellion reached Nero, the latter fainted. After recovering, he began to consider his options.*

[After he regained his senses, he] remained mute and insensible for a long while. Coming to himself, he tore his clothes and beat his forehead, crying that all was now over. . . . [He also] formed several appalling . . . schemes for dealing with the situation. Thus, he intended to depose all army commanders . . . and execute them on the charge that they were all involved in a single conspiracy. . . . He further considered poisoning the entire Senate at a banquet; and setting fire to the city . . . but first letting wild beasts loose in the streets to hinder citizens from saving themselves. However, he had to abandon these schemes . . . because he realized their impracticability in view of the military campaign soon forced on him.

individuals in the capital began plotting his death. On discovering these intrigues, Nero executed or exiled hundreds of people. It finally took an army revolt to eliminate him. Early in 68, Servius Galba, a provincial governor, was acclaimed emperor by his troops and threatened to march on Rome. The Senate and Praetorian Guard soon recognized Galba's authority, and Nero had to flee his palace. When some soldiers cornered him in a house, the tyrant stabbed himself in the throat and, as one ancient writer described it, "died, with eyes glazed and bulging from their sockets, a sight which horrified everybody present."[11]

Vespasian and Rome's "Rebirth"

Though Nero had been brutal and corrupt, his death did not immediately restore tranquility. Instead, it created a crisis the likes of which Rome had not faced since the civil wars of the late Republic. Galba was old and feeble. And after accepting the title of emperor from his troops, he made the mistake of refusing to pay them and the Praetorians some promised bonuses. So they murdered him. Meanwhile, other powerful generals were vying for ultimate power. They included Marcus Otho, Aulus Vitellius, and Titus Flavius Vespasianus (known as Vespasian). Because four men claimed the throne in 69, that year became known thereafter as "the year of the four emperors."

After a brief but bloody bout of civil strife, Vespasian emerged the victor. The combined reigns of Vespasian and his sons became known as the Flavian dynasty (after the name Flavius). Vespasian was a very different sort of ruler than Nero had been. The latter had traced his ancestry back to the aristocratic empire-builders

Augustus and Julius Caesar, whereas Vespasian came from a middle-class family of soldiers and civil servants and had worked his way up the army's chain of command. Once on the throne, Vespasian quickly demonstrated that he was not an autocrat at heart but rather a frugal, efficient bureaucrat interested only in restoring good government to Rome.

In fact, *restoration* became the principal theme of Vespasian's reign. He sought to create a new Rome, one of which all Romans could be proud, and to symbolize this goal he struck coins bearing the motto *Roma resurgens*, meaning "Rome reborn." Rebuilding Rome was a monumental task, as the great fire of 64 and the destruction wrought by the recent civil war had destroyed many of the city's structures. But Vespasian rose to the task and became one of Rome's most prolific builders. Suetonius recalls:

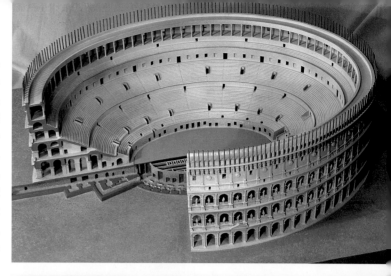

The photo shows the ruins of the Colosseum as they appear today; the painting shows how the structure originally looked.

> In Rome, which had been made unsightly by fires and collapsed buildings, Vespasian authorized anyone who pleased to take over the vacant sites, and build on them if the original owners failed to come forward. He personally inaugurated the restoration of the burned Capitol [temple of Jupiter], by collecting the first basketfull of rubble and carrying it away on his shoulders.[12]

Vespasian's greatest and most lasting achievement was initiating construction of the Colosseum (known in his day as the Amphitheater of the Flavians, reflecting that he and his sons erected it). Located in the heart of the capital, this huge facility for the presentation of gladiatorial combats and wild animal shows seated at least fifty thousand spectators.

Titus was a kind, caring, and popular ruler who died before he could realize his full potential.

Titus and Domitian

After a remarkably efficient and benevolent reign, Vespasian died in 79 and his sons, who succeeded him, for the most part continued his policies. This was par-

ticularly true of his immediate successor, Titus (whose full name was the same as his father's). Titus continued work on and inaugurated the Colosseum. But in his own time he was better known for his kindness and preoccupation with the welfare of his subjects. He frequently engaged ordinary people in conversation at the public games or in the bathhouses and intently listened to their grievances. According to Suetonius, he "had a rule never to dismiss any petitioner without leaving him some hope that his request would be favorably considered."[13]

The most famous incidents of Titus's brief reign were three catastrophes that struck Italy in rapid succession. One was the great eruption of Mt. Vesuvius in August 79, which destroyed the towns of Pompeii and Herculaneum. The second was a fire that destroyed a number of buildings in the capital. The third was a serious disease epidemic that caused much death and suffering in Rome. Titus reacted to these calamities by organizing large-scale relief efforts that greatly reduced the victims' suffering. He even donated some of his own belongings to furnish structures rebuilt after the fire.

When Titus died suddenly in 81 after ruling only two years, his brother, Domitian (Titus Flavius Domitianus), ascended the throne. The new emperor governed the economy and provinces efficiently and erected numerous fine buildings. But he lacked the easygoing manner and likable personality of his father and brother. Moody and distrustful of most people, Domitian also hated the senators and treated them with disrespect.

An Insecure, Unhappy Ruler

In an excerpt from his Chronicle of the Roman Emperors, *noted scholar Chris Scarre provides this informative summary of Domitian's descent into paranoia, which led to his reign of terror and assassination.*

Domitian was not a happy individual. He suffered from a sense of social inadequacy, and preferred to take a walk after dinner rather than sitting late into the night with his companions. He was also an exceedingly fearful man, who had the palace colonnades lined with white reflective marble so that he could see what was going on around him. . . . It was Domitian's deepening suspicion [that people were out to hurt him] . . . which eventually drove him to cruelty. . . . Goaded by paranoia . . . [in 93 he] turned upon senators, knights, and imperial officials alike, ordering executions or exile. The reign of terror had exactly the opposite effect to what Domitian had intended, for he did not even spare his personal staff and relations. . . . [A] conspiracy was hatched during the summer months of 96. . . . The conspirators were Domitian's own personal attendants, driven to seek safety in his murder.

Domitian, Titus's brother, was an effective administrator but suffered from mental and emotional problems.

Eventually, he made so many enemies in the capital that a palace plot was hatched against him, and it succeeded. He was assassinated in 96, ending the Flavian line of rulers.

Fortunately for the Roman Empire, its first century had been dominated by capable, honest rulers. The interludes of corruption and abuse perpetrated by Sejanus, Caligula, and Nero (and to a lesser degree Domitian in his last years) had been brief. And overall prosperity had remained intact. This trend would continue under Domitian's five successors, who would bring the Pax Romana and Roman civilization itself to their highest levels.

Chapter Three

Bread and Circuses: Attempts to Maintain Control

One of the major concerns of the Roman emperors in the first century A.D. and beyond was maintaining their great power over the state and the people. The army's backing was essential to this task. So each emperor endeavored to acquire and maintain the soldiers' allegiance.

But by itself controlling the military was not enough. Appeasing the "mob," as many Roman leaders flippantly called the masses of ordinary people, was also crucial. Rome and some other cities had large populations, including many poor and unemployed people. Also, because slaves did many of the menial tasks for Romans of all walks of life, large numbers of people had excess leisure time at their disposal. Not a few emperors and other leaders harbored the paranoid fear that the mob might use these spare hours to plot, riot, or even rebel.

To guard against such unwanted developments, the government evolved a policy intended to keep the masses of unemployed and idle people fed, busy, and hopefully reasonably happy. The policy was twofold. On the one hand, each emperor sponsored regular large-scale distributions of free bread and other foodstuffs to the poor. By the late first century A.D., as many as 150,000 urban Romans received such handouts at hundreds of distribution centers located across the capital city.

Roman leaders also spent huge sums subsidizing public festivals, shows, and games. These took place on official holidays, of which there were a great many—annually, about 115 in Augustus's time and more than 130 by the end of the first century. The government also learned it was wise policy to supply large-scale bathhouses where people of all walks of life could go to relax and entertain themselves.

This policy of appeasing the masses through both free food and a wide range of entertainments eventually became known as *panem et circenses*, or "bread and circuses."

For reference, modern scholars often quote a famous sarcastic and bitter remark by the first-century satirist Juvenal. "There's only two things that concern" the commoners, he said, "bread and [circus] games."[14] Less frequently cited but more penetrating was a similar statement by the second-century orator Marcus Cornelius Fronto:

> [The emperors know] that the Roman people are held in control principally by two things—free grain and shows— that political support depends as much on the entertainments as on matters of serious import, that neglect of serious problems does the greater harm, but neglect of entertainments brings damaging unpopularity, that gifts [from the emperor] are less eagerly and ardently longed for than shows, and finally, that gifts placate [appease] only the common people on the grain dole, singly and individually, but the shows placate everyone.[15]

An emperor and his family lounge in the royal box at the Colosseum. The games presented there were intended partly to keep the idle masses occupied.

Holidays and Feasts

The many public games, festivals, and feasts people attended to fill their leisure time were collectively referred to as *ludi*. Some *ludi* were religious celebrations honoring specific gods. The Vestalia, for example, celebrated on June 9, honored Vesta, goddess of the hearth. Other *ludi* were secular, such as the Parentalia, observed from February 13 to 21 to honor the memory of deceased parents.

Still other *ludi* began as religious ceremonies but later became more secular. The most notable example was the Ludi Romani, a fifteen-day festival held from September 5 to 19. In earlier centuries it had honored Rome's chief god, Jupiter, in his own temple. By the first century A.D., however, much of the religious significance of the celebration had disappeared. Public officials met in the temple for a party and banquet, and other people had feasts in their homes.

Whether it was a holiday feast or a dinner party staged on an ordinary day, a Roman banquet, especially in a well-to-do home, featured certain traditional customs involving social status as well as food and table manners.

Onlookers signal their approval as a religious procession moves through the streets on one of the many holidays celebrated during the early Empire.

A group of friends gathers for a modest banquet in a house in Pompeii. At the time, such parties were a major form of entertainment.

Guests were assigned to separate couches according to their status, for example. Those who enjoyed the highest status sat the closest to the host or guest of honor.

Social status was also defined in part by the food served at a banquet. The more numerous, varied, and expensive the dishes a host served, the more impressive he seemed to his guests. It was not unusual, therefore, for some people to spend more than they could afford on the food for such occasions, causing them to go into debt. Conversely, hosts often used food as a way of making sure that their guests knew their own social places. It was a common custom to serve a different grade or quality of food to different dinner guests, depending on their status. The host and his more distinguished guests ate the more expensive dishes, whereas people of lower status, especially freedmen (freed slaves), received cheaper, simpler fare.

Regardless of social position, all of those attending a banquet displayed certain table manners that would appear odd or even uncouth today. Most foods were eaten with the fingers, for example. (An exception was runny foods, such as soup,

"From the Egg to the Apples"

The fare at Rome's fancier feasts and dinner parties during the Empire reflected both a love of good food and the desire of hosts to impress their guests. Dinner (*cena*) was customarily served in three courses, collectively called *ab ovo usque ad malla* ("from the egg to the apples"). In the first course, *gustus*, the guests nibbled on appetizers, variously including lettuce, leeks, mint, mushrooms and other raw vegetables, along with olives, eggs, snails, sardines, and shellfish. The second and main course, *prima mensa*, featured cooked meats and vegetables. The most common meats were fowl (hens, geese, and other birds), fish, sows' udders, wild boar, lamb, and pork (the Romans' favorite meat). These dishes were frequently enhanced with rich sauces. The wealthier hosts sometimes imported exotic and expensive delicacies, including lobster, pheasant and pheasant brains, ostrich, peacocks and peacock brains, flamingo tongues, fish livers, and the eggs of eels. Finally, the third and last course, *secunda mensa*, was the dessert, most often consisting of fruit (pears, grapes, figs, and so forth), nuts, puddings, and honey cakes and other pastries.

These depictions of typical Roman foods are restorations of ancient mosaics found in the ruins of Pompeii.

Two chariots near the far turn in a reconstruction of a race in the Circus Maximus. This immense facility sat at least 150,000 people.

pudding, and eggs, which were eaten with a spoon.) Also, it was common for the guests to bring along their own napkins. With these they not only wiped their mouths but also wrapped up their leftovers to take home, the Roman equivalent of a "doggy bag." Among other table manners that would be frowned on today was belching. It may have been accepted among Romans as a polite gesture signifying satisfaction with the meal. People also routinely tossed their food scraps onto the floor. A number of surviving ancient mosaics show dining room floors littered with such refuse, which the host's slaves had to clean up when the feast was over.

Chariot Races

Many of Rome's holiday festivals were accompanied not only by feasts but also by public games. Rome's two most popular public entertainments were chariot racing and gladiatorial combats. The races usually took place in long oval-shaped

Gladiators grapple in the Pompeii Amphitheater. Not all fights ended in death, as many matches were declared draws.

facilities called circuses. The most spectacular example was the Circus Maximus in Rome, covering an area of some 2,000 by 700 feet (609 by 213m) and seating at least 150,000 people.

A day of chariot racing in the great circus began with a *pompa*, a colorful parade. Leading the way was the director of the games, who rode in a chariot and wore a purple toga. He was followed by various priests, public officials, the charioteers, and others, all decked out in fine clothes.

When the parade ended, the first race began. The drivers had to complete seven full laps (about 2.5 miles [4km]), during

which time they ruthlessly vied for every possible advantage. Each attempted to maneuver into the inside lane, against the racetrack's central spine (the *euripus*), since the distance of a lap in this position was somewhat shorter than in the outer lanes. The charioteers also attempted to sabotage one another by breaking the wheels or axles of rival chariots. This sometimes resulted in a "shipwreck," the crash of a chariot and its horses into a mass of twisted debris and broken bones.

As the emperors who sponsored the races knew, the suspense, danger, violence, and bloodletting that were part of this spectacle were guaranteed to draw and satisfy large crowds. Still, a few Romans viewed the races as lowbrow and pointless. One was Pliny the Younger, who says in one of his published letters:

> If they [the fans] were attracted by the speed of the horses or the drivers' skill one could account for it, but in fact it is the racing-colors they really support and care about. [Drivers from different teams, or stables, wore different colored shirts.] . . . Such is the popularity of a worthless shirt. . . . When I think of how this futile, tedious, monotonous business can keep them sitting endlessly in their seats, I take pleasure in the fact that their pleasure is not mine.[16]

Gladiatorial Fights

Pliny felt just as much disdain for gladiatorial combats, which were nearly as popular with crowds as the chariot races. The combats took place in amphitheaters, large oval structures with dirt arenas in the center. The Colosseum, built in Rome by the Flavian emperors, was the largest amphitheater in the Empire, measuring 620 by 513 feet (189 by 156m) and seating some fifty thousand people.

The gladiators who fought in the Colosseum included both men and women, though most were men. They were mainly prisoners, slaves, and criminals, although a few were free persons who volunteered. One motivation for the latter was the generous prize money the winners often received. Other volunteers were drawn by the physical challenge and appeal of danger or the prospect of becoming popular idols and sex symbols who could have their pick of pretty young girls.

There were numerous different types and categories of gladiator. The most common types brandished swords or lances, along with shields for protection. Others used nets to ensnare their opponents before stabbing them with spears. Still others fought on horseback or chariots and threw lassoes at their opponents.

Like a chariot race, a typical gladiatorial display began with a colorful parade in which the gladiators marched along with musicians and entertainers. Then the fighters drew lots to decide who would fight whom. Finally, the gladiators soberly raised their weapons toward the highest-ranking official present (usually either the emperor or the director of the games) and recited the phrase, "We who are about to die salute you!" The first scheduled pair of gladiators then fought. Although the combatants tried to kill each other, not all matches ended in death, as some were declared draws. It was also common for one gladiator to be wounded, appeal for mercy, and be spared by the emperor or other high official. (Sometimes, however, the appeal was denied, in which case the victor of the match slit the fallen person's throat.)

Animal Fights and Acts

The Roman masses were also attracted and appeased by games featuring fights between humans and beasts and between beasts and beasts. Generally termed *venationes*, or "hunts," they were originally minor spectacles presented in amphitheaters in the early morning, before the gladiatorial bouts. By the early years of the Empire, however, the hunts had become popular enough to warrant staging them in late afternoon, when more people attended the games.

The animals that took part in these spectacles came from the far corners of the Empire and often beyond. Among them were leopards, lions, tigers, bulls, elephants, ostriches, and crocodiles. Sometimes these beasts fought a "hunter," who carried a spear, sword, club, bow and arrow, or some other weapon. Other times, the animals were goaded to attack and fight one another. The same beasts were also used by the government to kill condemned prisoners in gory public executions held from time to time in the arenas.

In stark contrast to these gruesome displays, Roman crowds also greatly enjoyed trained animal acts. Among the more popular were monkeys dressed as soldiers and driving miniature chariots drawn by goats. Other celebrated attractions included lions that held rabbits or even mice in their jaws without harming them, bears that played ball, and a perennial crowd favorite—trained elephants.

The Public Baths

One drawback of the large-scale public games was that they were extremely

Fan Violence in a Roman Town

Most of the time, the fighting in the gladiatorial games appropriately took place in the arena. Occasionally, however, the violence spilled over into the audience, as shown in this excerpt from Tacitus's Annals, *documenting a serious riot that occurred in Pompeii's arena in A.D. 59, during Nero's reign.*

There was a serious fight between the inhabitants of two [neighboring] Roman settlements, Nuceria and Pompeii. It arose out of a trifling incident at a gladiatorial show given by Livineius Regulus. . . . During an exchange of taunts—characteristic of these disorderly country towns—abuse led to stone-throwing, and then swords were drawn. The people of Pompeii, where the show was held, came off best. Many wounded and mutilated Nucerians were taken to the capital [Rome]. Many bereavements, too, were suffered by parents and children. The emperor instructed the Senate to investigate the affair. The Senate passed it to the consuls. When they reported back, the Senate debarred Pompeii from holding any similar gathering for ten years. Illegal associations in the town were dissolved; and the sponsor of the show and his fellow-instigators of the disorders were exiled.

This painting shows a cutaway of the Stabian Baths in Pompeii. Such facilities had athletic fields, snack bars, and many other amenities.

expensive to stage; therefore, they were presented only on selected holidays or other special occasions. This left plenty of leisure time for Romans to fill with other activities, including regular visits to the public baths. In fact, from the first century B.C. on, attending the baths was probably the most common Roman pastime, one that people of nearly all walks of life enjoyed.

To accommodate these crowds, the government erected many public bathhouses (although some were privately built and run as well). By the middle of Augustus's reign, the capital alone had more than 170 bathhouses; by the late first century there were perhaps double that number; and by the Empire's last century, Rome boasted more than 900 bathhouses. These facilities ranged widely in size, attractiveness, and quality of service. Some were small and dirty. Others were enormous, palacelike structures adorned with magnificent art treasures. Among the latter were the baths of Agrippa, Nero, Titus, Trajan, Caracalla, Diocletian, and Constantine. Caracalla's baths, erected in the early third century A.D., took some nine thousand workmen more than five years to complete.

As for how often people attended the baths, it depended in large degree on

A Condemnation of Communal Bathing

In Rome's earlier centuries, men and women never bathed together. After coming into close contact with the Greeks in the second century B.C., however, the Romans began to adopt the custom of communal bathing. Many Romans resisted this at first. A common view was that Greek luxuries and social customs, including public bathing and competing in athletics, were soft, unmanly, and frivolous and would surely corrupt the moral fiber of Roman society. The first-century historian Tacitus later summed up this attitude in his Annals, *writing:*

Traditional morals, already gradually deteriorating, have been utterly ruined by this imported laxity [moral looseness]! It makes everything potentially corrupting and corruptible flow into the capital, [as] foreign influences demoralize our young men into shirkers, gymnasts, and [sexual] perverts. . . . Good behavior has no time left for it. In these promiscuous crowds, debauchees [immoral people] are emboldened to practice by night the lusts they have imagined by day.

personal preference. Some people went once a week or even more infrequently, but large numbers of Romans attended every day or even several times a day. The sheer number and size of the bathhouses in Rome and other cities implies a large number of regular customers. And the cost was certainly low enough for even the poorest Romans to attend often. The entrance fee for adults was equivalent to pocket change today, and children got in for free.

The larger bathhouses featured a series of connected rooms, beginning with lobbies, reception and meeting rooms, and chambers for undressing and dressing. Patrons then made their way into a warm room without a bath, where they remained until they started perspiring. Some went on to a hot room with one or more pools of hot water. Others chose instead to visit a cold room featuring one or more pools of cold water. Other popular alternatives were a saunalike dry room and an oil room, where people enjoyed massages.

Patrons of the bathhouses had other options as well. They could do laps in a large swimming pool, exercise in gyms, play handball, dine in onsite snackbars, or lounge in quiet reading rooms. In short, these public facilities were places where people could find relaxation and entertainment for a pleasant hour or an entire day. It is no wonder that the emperors saw fit to build them and thereby help to keep the masses busy, out of trouble, and under control.

Chapter Four

The Five Good Emperors: Rome at Its Zenith

Following the assassination of Domitian, last of the Flavians, Rome entered an extended period dominated by the rule of five men. History came to call Nerva, Trajan, Hadrian, Antoninus Pius, and Marcus Aurelius the "five good emperors." This name was well earned, for they were extremely capable and enlightened rulers who presided over the Roman Empire at its height of size and prosperity. Although they made no attempt to restore republican government, they reestablished an efficient working relationship with the Senate. The five good emperors also instituted numerous social reforms and laws designed to protect the poor, the underprivileged, and even slaves. Perhaps most importantly, they ensured a healthy economy by in effect extending the Pax Romana nearly another century. There *were* rebellions and defensive and offensive border wars during this period. But the many lands making up the Empire remained largely peaceful, safe, and pros-

perous. As the great eighteenth-century English historian Edward Gibbon famously sums it up:

> If a man were called upon to fix the period in the history of the world during which the condition of the human race was most happy and prosperous, he would without hesitation name that which elapsed from the [accession of Nerva to the death of Aurelius]. . . . Their united reigns are possibly the only period of history in which the happiness of a great people was the sole object of government.[17]

Respect for the Senate Is Restored

The first of the good emperors, Marcus Cocceius Nerva, was a senator in his sixties when he ascended the throne in the year 96. Unlike his predecessors, he neither sought nor even dreamed of attaining

The Five Good Emperors

Trajan

Nerva

Hadrian

Antoninus Pius

Marcus Aurelius

imperial power. The conspirators who had eliminated Domitian gained the backing of most senators, who had come to hate the emperor for treating them with disrespect. And no one wanted a rerun of the violent rivalries among army generals that had followed Nero's demise. So the Senate chose as emperor the surprised Nerva, a civilian and one of the more capable and respected lawmakers in Rome.

Nerva swiftly established himself as a sincere and able ruler. Having been a senator, he realized that good relations between the emperor and Senate would benefit everyone. So he returned to Augustus's wise policy of treating the senators with respect. Nerva promised never to execute a senator. And although he was firmly in control, he allowed the Senate the appearance of running the government. Nerva also initiated a series of social reforms similar to modern welfare systems, which his successors would continue and enlarge. One of these programs was a fund to help orphans and poor children.

The weak point of Nerva's reign consisted of his uneasy relationship with the Praetorian Guard. Its members were the only Romans who missed Domitian (because he had given them a pay raise),

A crowd begins to gather in the Forum of Trajan, inaugurated in A.D. 115. This architectural masterpiece adjoined the Forum of Augustus.

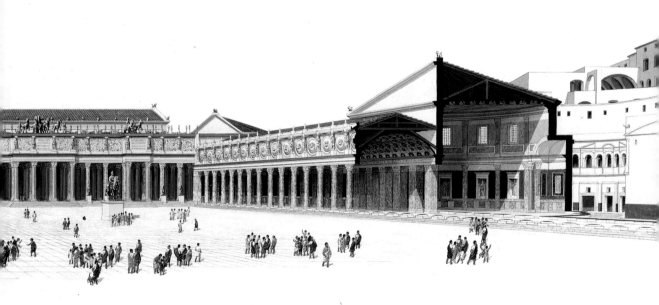

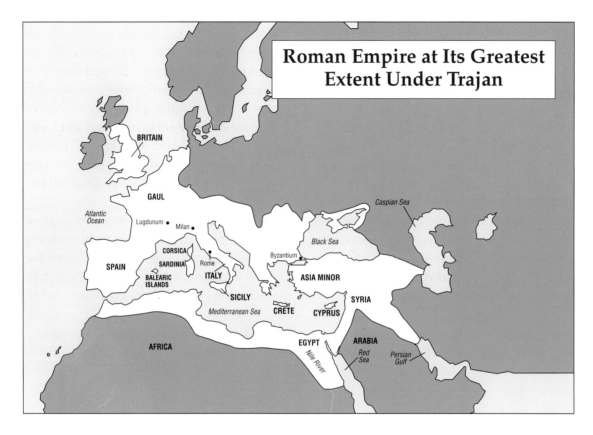

Roman Empire at Its Greatest Extent Under Trajan

and on one occasion they openly defied the new emperor. To appease both the Praetorian Guard and the army, and thereby maintain peace and stability, Nerva wisely decided on an unprecedented move. In October 97, while still on the throne, he formally adopted as his son and successor Marcus Ulpius Trajanus (Trajan), governor of the province of Upper Germany and commander of several army legions. This satisfied the military elements and ensured a smooth succession when Nerva passed on.

Trajan Expands the Realm

Nerva's timing in choosing a successor proved fortunate. In January 98, only three months after naming Trajan as his heir,

Nerva died of natural causes. The planned succession proceeded in an orderly fashion, and the forty-two-year-old Trajan became emperor with both the army's and Senate's blessings.

Significantly, Trajan hailed from Spain, making him the first emperor born outside Italy. This showed that the old image of the provinces as foreign territories inferior in status to Italy was rapidly disappearing. From the second century onward, most Romans viewed the realm as a single political unit composed of many diverse regions.

Like Nerva, Trajan was a capable ruler whose primary interest was the welfare of the Empire and its people. The new emperor showed the Senate every courtesy, often socializing with its members and asking their advice. He also carried on his predecessor's domestic policies, increasing state funds for poor children and other needy individuals. In addition, Trajan's economic administration was extremely sound. As a result, he found the money to launch the largest public building program Rome had seen since Augustan days. All over the Empire he erected aqueducts, harbors, canals, and many fine roads.

Trajan's most important accomplishment, however, was his expansion of the realm. Most prior emperors had followed Augustus's policy of remaining content with existing Roman borders. But Trajan wanted to match or even surpass his personal hero, Julius Caesar, by aggressively expanding Rome's horizons. Like so many other Romans, Trajan believed that he was doing the "barbarians" a favor by subduing and "civilizing" them. In a series of brilliant military campaigns between 101 and 107, he conquered Dacia (now Romania), lying west of the Black Sea. He then made the area a province. To celebrate these deeds, the emperor erected a 110-foot-high (34m) column in Rome. Covered with magnificent carved reliefs depicting his campaigns, the monument still stands almost completely intact.

Not content with his Dacian conquests, between 114 and 116 Trajan marched his legions into the lands of Armenia and Mesopotamia (located east and southeast of the Black Sea). These also became Roman provinces. The Empire was now larger than it had ever been or ever would be. It stretched from the Atlantic Ocean in the west to the Persian Gulf in the east; and from north Africa in the south to central

Praise for Rome's Accomplishments

The second-century Greek writer Aelius Aristides composed a long speech of praise (excerpted here from Lewis and Reinhold's Roman Civilization, Sourcebook II) *intended to sum up the overall achievement of Rome in the Pax Romana. He said in part:*

There is nothing on earth like it [the Empire]. . . . The whole world speaks in unison. . . in praying this Empire may last for all time. . . . Every place is full of gymnasia, fountains, gateways, temples, shops, and schools. . . . Gifts never stop flowing from you to the cities . . . [that] shine in radiance and beauty. . . . Only those outside your Empire, if there are any, are fit to be pitied for losing such blessings. . . .Greek and [non-Greek] can now readily go wherever they please with their property or without it. . . . You have surveyed the whole world, built bridges of all sorts across rivers, cut down mountains to make paths for chariots, filled the deserts with hostels, and civilized it all with system and order.

Britain in the north. In total, this colossal political unit encompassed some 3.5 million square miles (9 million sq. km) and more than 100 million people.

Trajan and the Christians

While Trajan was an aggressive conqueror, he was also a fair and compassionate ruler. His lenient treatment of the Christians was an example. Partly because the Christians swore allegiance to Jesus Christ rather than to the emperor, and also because they scorned all gods but their own, most Romans viewed them as a dangerous, even criminal element. (The Romans were willing to allow the Christians to worship their own god; however, Romans demanded tolerance and respect for all gods, which the Christians refused to give.) As a result, periodic persecutions of Christians had occurred since Nero's time.

Although Trajan did not fully understand Christian religious views, he felt he knew enough to judge that they were not a serious threat to the Empire. The emperor's feelings on the matter have fortunately been preserved in a series of letters he exchanged with Pliny the Younger, whom he had sent to investigate domestic affairs in Asia Minor. Pliny told Trajan:

> I have never been present at the examination of Christians. Consequently, I do not know the nature of the extent of the punishments usually meted out to them. . . . I have therefore postponed any further examination and hastened to consult you.

Trajan answered in part:

> You have followed the right course of procedure, my dear Pliny, in your examination of the . . . Christians, for it is impossible to lay down a general rule [for dealing with them]. These people must not be hunted out. If they are brought before you and the charge against them is proved, they must be punished. But in the case of anyone who denied that he is a Christian . . . he is to be pardoned as a result of his repentance.[18]

Trajan's treatment of the Christians was significant. He did not openly tolerate them. But by allowing them to be pardoned rather than punished, he foreshadowed future toleration of their sect.

The Distinguished Traveler

Trajan ensured that his fair policies would continue after his death by choosing as his heir Publius Aelius Hadrianus (Hadrian), an honest, intelligent man who was also a distinguished army officer. When Trajan died in 117, Hadrian, then forty-one, ascended the throne. Fulfilling his mentor's expectations, the new emperor immediately devoted all his energies to running a fair and efficient government. Among Hadrian's many reforms was a requirement that all senators and many other public officials receive training in government administration. In this way, he built up a large pool of well-trained officials to carry out his policies.

Hadrian also expanded the welfare system. He opened free schools for poor

Hadrian's Defenses

Although Hadrian opted for a smaller, more easily manageable realm, he did pour a lot of time and money into building defenses of existing borders. For instance, he greatly reinforced and expanded the realm's northern defenses, which kept the Germanic and other "barbarian" tribes at bay. These defenses consisted of wooden palisades backed up by forts at intervals. They stretched for some 2,500 miles (4,023km), from the North Sea in the northwest to the Black Sea in the east. Even more impressive was the defensive wall Hadrian erected in Britain to protect the island's Roman-controlled lands from the Scottish tribes in the north. Hadrian's Wall, as it came to be known, was constructed of stone. It stood 16 feet (5m) high, featured a moat 26 feet (8m) wide and 10 feet (3m) deep, and stretched for some 73 miles (117km). Supporting these defenses were eighty small castlelike forts spaced about a mile apart and 160 defensive towers. Hadrian's Wall was so well constructed that large portions of it are still intact.

The remains of a section of Hadrian's wall, in Britain, can be seen at right; below is a restoration of how it looked in its prime.

This ivory carving depicts the benevolent ruler Antoninus Pius (sitting at upper right).

children and strengthened laws protecting slaves from abuse. A later Roman chronicle records:

> He prohibited the killing of slaves by their owners and ordered that they should be sentenced by judges if they deserved it. He prohibited the sale of a male or female slave to a pimp or gladiatorial trainer without cause being given. Workhouses for slaves and freedmen [freed slaves] he abolished.[19]

Hadrian did disagree with his predecessor in one area—the size of the Empire. The new emperor felt that it had become too large to administer efficiently. So he decided to give up the new provinces of Armenia and Mesopotamia. Hadrian based this and other provincial policies on firsthand information gathered in extensive travels throughout the realm. After his visit to Britain in 121, he ordered a long defensive wall to be built to keep the native tribes of Scotland from harassing the local Roman province (Britannia). After visits to Greece in 125 and 129, the emperor became a fervent devotee of Greek culture. And he spent large sums of money restoring Greek temples and other fine structures that had fallen into disrepair.

Rome's Potential Fulfilled?

Shortly before his death from illness in 138, Hadrian named as his successor fifty-one-year-old Titus Aurelius Antoninus, a former provincial governor. Antoninus was one of the most capable and perhaps the most humane of all Roman rulers. He was so ethical, honest, and sincere that the Senate bestowed on him the titles of Pius, meaning "Devout," and Optimus Princeps, "the Best of Princes." His successor, Marcus Aurelius, later said of him:

> He showed sobriety in all things and firmness, and never any mean thoughts or action. . . . There was in him nothing harsh nor implacable, nor violent . . . but [instead] he examined all things

. . . as if he had an abundance of time, and without confusion, in an orderly way, vigorously and consistently.[20]

Partly because Antoninus was so dedicated to good and fair rule, the Empire reached the height of its prosperity during his reign. He ran the economy so well, in fact, that at the end of his reign he left a surplus of 2.7 billion *sesterces* (the equivalent of hundreds of millions of dollars today). Antoninus also carried on his predecessors' social welfare programs and showed an unprecedented degree of sympathy for oppressed groups. For example, he increased the severity of punishments for owners who killed their slaves. Antoninus seemed so just a ruler to so many people that writers of many nationalities heaped praises on him and the realm during his reign. In the most famous of the surviving panegyrics (formal speeches of praise), a Greek named Aelius Aristides exclaimed, "Every place is full of gymnasia, fountains, gateways, temples, shops, and schools! . . . You [Romans] have surveyed the whole world . . . and civilized it all with system and order!"[21]

The Philosopher-Emperor

Panegyrics like that of Aristides always omitted any negative aspects of the rulers or institutions they praised. Certainly Antoninus's reign witnessed its share of local rebellions and other minor troubles. Yet when Antoninus died peacefully of natural causes at age eighty-five in March 161, Roman law and order, prosperity, military power, and civilized culture appeared invincible. Most people at the time assumed that these qualities would also be long-lasting, perhaps even eternal.

Yet this was not to be. In the years following Antoninus's passing, Rome began

Marcus Aurelius's Stoic Writings

Among the core Stoic principles Marcus Aurelius discusses and promotes in his book Meditations *(excerpted here from George Long's translation), is that all living things are linked and empowered by an intelligent force that underlies nature's fabric.*

Frequently consider the connection of all things in the universe and their relation to one another. For in a manner, all things are implicated with one another, and all in this way are friendly to one another. . . . In the things that are held together by nature there is within and abides in them the power which made them. Therefore, the more fit it is to reverence this power, and to think that if you live and act according to its will, everything in you is in conformity to intelligence. And thus also in the universe the things which belong to it are in conformity to intelligence.

to experience some serious problems. Shortly after ascending the throne at age forty, Antoninus's successor, Marcus Aelius Aurelius, was obliged to defend the Empire's borders. First, the Parthians, who dwelled in the region of the Persian Gulf, invaded some of Rome's eastern provinces. In the early 160s, Roman forces defeated the intruders and restored order. But during the campaign some of the soldiers caught a deadly disease, possibly smallpox. Returning veterans spread the illness across the Empire and millions died. Some frightened people blamed the Christians for the plague and attacked them. At heart a peaceful, kind man, the emperor disapproved of these persecutions, but he could not control angry mobs all over the realm.

Marcus Aurelius also had no control over, or even knowledge of, the mass migrations of tribal peoples that had been occurring for years in northern Europe. In 167, large numbers of Germans spilled into Rome's northern provinces. And in the fifteen years that followed, the emperor personally led armies in defensive campaigns against the invaders.

During these troubled times, Aurelius, an honest, just, and hardworking man, did his best to rule his vast domain efficiently. A scholar and thinker as well as a statesman, he tried to govern according to the tenets of Stoicism. This school of thought, which had been popular among Roman intellectuals for more than three centuries, held that all things that happen are guided by a sort of divine providence. And humans should live in harmony with nature, which is also governed by divine reason. A talented writer, Aurelius recorded his thoughts in a book titled *Meditations*. "Keep yourself simple, good, pure, [and] serious," he wrote. "Reverence the gods and help men."[22]

A Changing World

By all accounts, the last of the five good emperors, true to his personal beliefs, did his best to help as many of his subjects as possible. Aurelius was as thoughtful and evenhanded as any ruler could ever hope or claim to be. But during his reign the world he and his predecessors had known was changing rapidly. Moreover, both the Roman government and Roman society were ill prepared to deal with mounting forces that had the potential to rupture the Empire's very fabric. More and larger invasions began to threaten the borders. Also, the state found it increasingly difficult to both administer and defend such an enormous domain. At the same time, serious economic problems began taking an awful toll on the realm and its inhabitants.

As a result of these ominous trends, the years following Marcus Aurelius's death in 180 witnessed the steady spread of a marked change of attitude among large numbers of Romans. For the first time in living memory, they realized that Rome might not be invincible. And they were afraid.

Chapter Five

The Anarchy: Rome on the Brink of Collapse

After the passing of Marcus Aurelius, last of the so-called five good emperors, Rome's political and economic problems rapidly increased. Nearly a century of decline and eventually severe crisis followed. During the years of crisis, lasting from about 235 to the late 270s, peace and prosperity were shattered and the Empire approached the brink of total collapse. Modern historians refer to the period variously as "the Anarchy," "the century of crisis," "the military monarchy," and "the age of the soldier-emperors."

Whatever the era is called, the crisis that dominated it had several dimensions and causes. First, there was a serious shortage of good leadership. In contrast to the honest and capable rulers of the second century, most of those who succeeded them were ambitious, brutal, and/or incompetent. They had little or no concept of how to deal with the serous problems the realm faced.

The Anarchy also witnessed a dire military crisis. In the face of large-scale inva-sions from the north and east that threat-ened to rip the Empire apart, the army proved disorganized and sometimes even disloyal. Frequently the army or the Praetorian Guard ran amok, choosing and disposing of emperors at will.

Another important dimension of the cri-sis was economic. War and political insta-bility disrupted trade, and the decline of farming, which had been going on for some time, began to take a toll on the food supply. The government also spent too much money and overtaxed or placed other burdens on the populace in an effort to make up its losses.

As a result of these and other problems, law and order often broke down, poverty increased sharply, and, for many Romans, life in the Empire became miserable, dan-gerous, and uncertain. Eventually, Rome managed to recover substantially from the disasters of this period. But it did so at a price of a radically reorganized govern-ment and society. The Roman realm that

A bust shows Commodus dressed as the heroic strongman Hercules, with whom this emperor strongly identified.

emerged from the Anarchy was more unstable and far less prosperous and happy than the one that had thrived during the Pax Romana.

The Need for Strong Leadership

These striking contrasts between the Rome of the Pax Romana and that of the third century naturally raise the question of how a strong and stable empire could have undergone so extensive and rapid a decline. Although many factors eventually contributed to this decline, one of the more pronounced and far-reaching was poor leadership. For example, though a fine ruler in his own right, Marcus Aurelius made a serious mistake that would have negative consequences later. Namely, he broke the tradition begun by Nerva in which each emperor named a competent administrator as the heir to the throne and adopted him as his son. Instead, perhaps out of a sense of family loyalty, Aurelius chose his biological son, Commodus, who became emperor in 180 at the age of eighteen or nineteen.

Commodus possessed a character almost exactly opposite to that of his father and other recent emperors. Vain, selfish, and spoiled, the new emperor often neglected his governmental responsibilities and spent large sums of public money on his own luxuries. A fourth-century chronicler captured the squalor of both Commodus's character and imperial court:

> He would drink till dawn and squander the resources of the Roman Empire. In the evening he flitted through the taverns to the brothels [houses of prostitution]. . . . Commodus . . . killed his sister Lucilla. . . . Then, having debauched [seduced] his other sisters . . . he even gave one of the concubines [mistresses] the name of his mother. His wife, whom he had caught in adultery, he drove out, then banished her, and subsequently killed her.[23]

As for his foreign policy, what little there was of it, Commodus reversed his father's policy of resisting the influx of barbarian tribes into the northern provinces. Unwilling to interrupt his pleasures in Rome with time-consuming military campaigns, the young ruler struck a deal with the tribes. In exchange for peace, he allowed some of their members to settle in the border provinces and even encouraged some thirteen thousand barbarians to enlist in the Roman army. This angered most generals and other high officials, who felt that Rome needed to ensure its future safety by keeping the barbarians out.

Commodus also made enemies by maintaining a reign of terror in the capital. He employed many spies and ordered hundreds of people executed for trivial offenses. Few if any were surprised or sorry when a palace assassination plot succeeded, ending his corrupt reign in 192.

The Rule of the Severi

Many Romans no doubt assumed that with the despot dead the Empire's leadership would settle back into the more stable and productive mode of the "good" emperors. But they were wrong. The five years following Commodus's passing witnessed a series of chaotic and often bloody power struggles. First, his immediate successors, Pertinax and Didius Julianus, reigned only three months and sixty-six days respectively before suffering the same fate he had suffered. A civil war ensued in which several army generals in various sectors of the realm claimed the throne. The strongest of these contenders was Septimius Severus, who emerged victorious in 197.

Severus was a stern, strong, and skilled general who managed to restore order and keep the barbarians on their own side of the northern borders. But he had little understanding of the Empire's serious internal problems, which were steadily worsening. The economy had weakened over the preceding decades, due to such factors as declining population (partly attributable to the plague of the 160s) and a reduction of agricultural output, which caused sporadic food shortages and rising food prices. A steadily diminishing volume of trade also took a toll.

Perhaps most destructive of all was monetary inflation caused by devaluation of the coinage. A growing lack of gold and silver forced the government to mint coins containing cheaper alloys, and this lessened the value of the money. For example, the denarius, a common Roman coin, was worth only about one-fortieth as much in A.D. 200 as it was at the beginning of the Pax Romana.

Severus failed to solve any of these problems. In fact, he actually made some of them worse. For instance, he ordered another decrease in the amount of silver in coins, which further devaluated money. This not only hindered trade and decreased people's buying power, but it also made his expensive military reforms harder to implement. He increased the army's size, creating a force of perhaps four hundred thousand men, and also raised the soldiers' pay. His successors maintained these large forces, while money became increasingly worthless. One result was that the next six decades saw the military pay and supply system buckle and finally break down.

An ardent militarist to the end, Severus is famous for the advice he gave his sons, Caracalla and Geta, on his deathbed in 211: "Enrich the soldiers [but] scorn everybody else."[24] For the most part, they and the other Severi (members of Severus's dynasty), who held sway over Rome until 235, followed this shortsighted counsel. Caracalla, Severus's immediate successor, was a poor administrator who was murdered by one of his own bodyguards in 217. He was succeeded by Macrinus (who probably helped engineer the assassination plot), Elagabalus, and Alexander Severus. All were ineffective rulers and ended up being assassinated or removed from power.

The Founder of the Severan Dynasty

Members of the Severan family ruled Rome from 193 to 235. Their patriarch, so to speak, Lucius Septimius Severus, was born at Lepcis Magna (in north Africa). As a young man he rose to high government posts, including quaestor, tribune of the people, and praetor. In 184 he became governor of one of the Gallic provinces and in 191 of Upper Pannonia, where he still resided when the emperor Commodus's death ignited a contest for the throne. Severus was proclaimed emperor by his troops and marched them to Rome. But other strong leaders, including Pescennius Niger, wanted to be emperor, and he had to defeat them before his position was completely secure. Severus accomplished this task by 196. From 197 to 199, he fought and defeated the Parthians and secured the province of Mesopotamia. In 208 he and his eldest son, Caracalla, invaded Caledonia (Scotland), which turned out to be an indecisive operation. And three years later, in the British town of York, Severus died. It is said that on his deathbed he told his sons to enrich and appease the soldiers at the expense of everyone else.

Septimius Severus was a tough, skilled soldier who fought his way to the throne.

Great Crisis of the 3rd Century

Picts
Celts
Londinium
Allamanni
Vandals
Ostrogoths
Quadi
Visigoths
Argentorate
Postumus's Gallic Empire
Armenia
Byzantium
Empire of Palmyra
Rome
Persia
Athens
Palmyra
Carthage
Alexandria

Areas Temporarily Independent
Area Abandoned in Mid-Century
Foreign Nation
Areas Subject to Barbarian Invasion
Legion Stations (214 A.D.)

Invaders Threaten the Realm

The weakness and instability of Roman leadership under the later Severi, as well as the problems they faced, proved merely a foretaste of what followed them. For the next half-century the Empire was threatened by invaders from the north and east. Meanwhile, the government was often in a state of turmoil or outright civil war; trade continued to decline; many soldiers, unable to rely on government pay, looted at will; and poverty and crime were rampant. Between 235 and 284 more than fifty rulers, most of them generals backed by their troops, claimed the throne. Although about half of them were formally acknowledged as emperors, perhaps only eighteen had any legitimate claim. Their average reign was 2.5 years, and all but one died by assassination or other violent means.

It was foolhardy and self-defeating, of course, for Roman rulers and generals to fight one another while they tried to beat back foreign invaders. But this is precisely what they did. And the Empire paid a terrible price in death, ruin, and misery. The first series of invasions came in the 230s as German tribes renewed their attacks on the Danube frontier, an area that remained under nearly constant siege for many years to come. Other tribes raided Gaul and even managed to penetrate into Spain, Greece, and Italy's Po Valley. The

An ancient Persian relief sculpture shows King Shapur I (on the horse) establishing dominance over Valerian (on bended knee).

government only barely managed to beat back the latter incursion, suffering large losses of men and supplies in the process.

Meanwhile, the embattled emperors and generals faced attacks on the realm's eastern borders. In the early 240s the newly crowned Sassanian king, Shapur I, began raiding Roman towns. (The Sassanians had recently revived the old Persian Empire, in what are now Iraq and Iran.) These assaults grew increasingly bold until, in 253 or 254, his forces overran Antioch, in Syria, one of the Empire's largest and most prosperous cities. Thousands of Antioch's inhabitants were deported to Persia, where they became slaves.

The emperor Valerian (reigned 253–260) led an expedition against the Sassanians in the late 250s and enjoyed some success at first. But in 260 he met with disaster. After his army had been decimated by an out-break of plague and surrounded by Shapur's troops, Valerian made the mistake of agreeing to a face-to-face meeting with the Persian monarch. During the negotiations, Shapur treacherously took the Roman leader and his officers prisoner. For the rest of his life Valerian remained in captivity, forced to crouch down to let Shapur step on his back when mounting his horse.

Old Traditions and Loyalties Steadily Fade

Not surprisingly, the incessant raids, invasions, and civil wars of this period of near-anarchy disrupted ordinary Romans' daily lives. Public works and commerce came to a near standstill, and many areas suffered from periodic bouts of famine and disease epidemics. The German and Persian invaders caused much death and destruction, of course. But just as damaging was the havoc created when Roman soldiers attacked, robbed, raped, and otherwise abused their own countrymen. An excerpt from the history penned by a writer of the period, Herodian (probably of Syrian birth), describes how the emperor Maximinus's troops ransacked the Roman city of Aquileia in 238:

> Finding the houses of the suburbs deserted [the Aquileians having fled], they cut down all the vines and trees, set some on fire, and made a shambles of the once-thriving countryside. . . . After destroying all this to the root, the army pressed on to the walls . . . and strove to demolish at least some part of the wall, so that they might break in and sack everything, razing the city and leaving the land a deserted pasturage.[25]

The Empire's inhabitants experienced a multitude of other problems, combining to make everyday life difficult and uncertain. In addition to paying high taxes, large numbers of people were required to supply Roman troops with food, clothing, and other supplies. These and similar pressures caused the traditional order of Roman life to change profoundly during the third century. The late, great modern scholar A.H.M. Jones described it this way:

> At one end of the scale peasants began deserting their holdings, either moving to another landlord who offered better terms, or abandoning agriculture altogether for the towns or for a career of banditry. . . . At the other end of the scale, a large number of senatorial families were killed off or reduced

Slaves of the Soil

One of the more troubling aspects of Roman society in the late second century and most of the third century was declining agriculture. More and more small farmers, unable to compete with the large farming estates (the *latifundia*), owned by wealthy individuals or the state, abandoned their fields. Many of these land tracts thereafter remained uncultivated for long periods of time. Meanwhile, the out-of-work farmers became part of a growing class of agrarian poor. Some migrated to the cities and lived on free bread distributed by the government; others remained on the land and became *coloni,* low-paid tenant workers on the larger farms. Desperate, they became financially dependent on their employers, who often took advantage of legal procedures to bind the *coloni* and their descendants to the same jobs for generations. Saddled with a status halfway between that of free persons and slaves, these tenant workers became known as "slaves of the soil."

The Goths

Among Rome's most formidable enemies in its later centuries, the Goths played a prominent role in the disruptions of the period known as the Anarchy. A tribal people, the Goths originally inhabited the region around the Vistula River, south of the Baltic Sea in what is now Poland. Sometime in the late second century A.D. they began a mass migration that led them to the Roman Empire's northern borders by the early 230s. A series of emperors, among them Philip the Arab and Decius, fought them. But the Goths proved too strong and determined. In 251 they defeated and killed Decius, and in the next twenty years they raided the Balkans and Asia Minor at will, inflicting widespread damage. The tide turned against the Goths during the reigns of Claudius II (268–270), who earned the name "Gothicus" for defeating them, and Aurelian (270–275), who beat them severely and pushed them back to the Danube. For a century thereafter, the Goths posed no serious threat to Roman territory. But they were destined to play a crucial role in the large-scale invasions that would plague Rome in the late fourth century.

An army of Goths slays the emperor Decius. The Goths were among the more formidable barbarian groups that threatened the Empire.

to poverty by the executions and confiscations [of property]. . . . On all sides the old traditions and the old loyalties were fading . . . the spirit of civic patriotism was fast vanishing in the middle class, the discipline of the troops was decaying, and there was nothing to take their place.[26]

A Striking Reversal

By the mid-260s, disunity, chaos, enemy incursions, economic decline, and a deterioration of the social order appeared to spell the end of the old Roman world. However, the same resiliency and spirit of determination that had pulled Rome back from the brink of doom on many occasions in its long history once more came to the fore. Beginning in 268 a series of strong military leaders took control and, as Michael Grant terms it, "In one of the most striking reversals in world history, Rome's foes were hurled back."[27]

First, the emperor Claudius II (268–270) inflicted a crushing defeat on the Germanic Alamanni tribe in the autumn of 268. And in the following year he campaigned successfully against another strong barbarian group, the Goths (an effort that won

him the title of "Gothicus.") Aurelian (270–275) also defeated the Alamanni, along with a newly arrived tribe, the Vandals. In addition, he built a defensive wall around the imperial capital 12 miles (19km) in circumference, 12 feet (3.6m) thick, and 20 feet (6.1m) high. Then, two of his successors, Probus and Carus, defeated more invaders, further helping to restore the unity of the realm.

The shrewdest, most talented, and by far most successful of this group of strong military emperors emerged in 284. In that year the young emperor Numerian was murdered by one of his own officers, Arrius Aper, while leading his army home from a campaign against the Sassanians. The soldiers promptly selected the head of the household cavalry, one Diocles, to carry out the punishment. Diocles did so in a bold way, stabbing Aper to death in full view of the assembled troops. They then proceeded to proclaim him emperor, after which he changed his name to Diocletian. Under his guidance, the Empire would continue its recovery from the Anarchy and enjoy a fresh start, although this new Rome would be a harsher, graver, less hopeful place than it had ever been.

Chapter Six

Rule by Sword and Cross: The Later Empire

After his position on the throne was secure, Diocletian initiated a series of political, administrative, and economic reforms designed to put the Empire back on its feet. The new Roman realm that emerged under his guidance, which modern historians often refer to as the Later Empire, was indeed more orderly than the deeply troubled one that had recently almost collapsed. Yet the new Rome was, overall, a more regimented and in some ways grimmer place in which to live than the Rome that had existed before the Anarchy.

These developments were bound to affect the way people saw themselves and their society. Indeed, as a result of the century of crisis and the reordering of society that followed, the Roman populace underwent a significant change of attitude. Some abandoned the old belief that Rome was a special place endorsed by the gods and came to see a certain level of misery and uncertainty as inevitable. Others searched for meaning and comfort in life by embracing new religious ideas. Under these conditions, Christianity, with its promise of happiness in the life to come, found fertile soil in which to grow. After more than two centuries of persecution and struggles for new converts, the Christians rapidly increased in numbers in the Later Empire. Eventually, even the emperors converted to the faith. These developments profoundly affected the nature of Roman institutions and life.

Diocletian's Reforms
In fact, strong indications that life would be different in the post-Anarchy Roman world came well before Christianity's meteoric rise, in the extensive reforms introduced by Diocletian. First, hoping to restore the prestige the throne had largely lost in recent years, he overhauled the Roman court. Diocletian demanded to be called *dominus* (lord) and ordered that anyone approaching must bow low and kiss

his robe. He also filled the Roman court with elaborate ceremony and layers of guards and spies, creating an air of awe and superstition that discouraged open dissent and assassination plots.

In addition, Diocletian launched a series of attempted economic reforms. One of these addressed the fact that, because of devaluation of coins and rampant inflation, money had become nearly worthless. To stabilize the money supply, Diocletian ordered the minting of pure gold and silver coins. Supplies of these precious metals were still very limited, however; so the few valuable coins that were circulated were snatched up by those who could afford them and privately hoarded. The result was that the government had no

Diocletian's Economic Edict

This excerpt from the opening section of Diocletian's famous edict on prices (quoted in Lewis and Reinhold's Roman Civilization, Sourcebook II) *calls on all Romans to observe the new law and warns that those who do not will be punished.*

It is our pleasure . . . that the prices listed in the subjoined [attached] summary be observed in the whole of our Empire. And every person shall take note that the liberty to exceed them at will has been ended. . . . Anyone who resists the measures of this statute shall be subject to a capital penalty for daring to do so. . . . We therefore urge the loyalty of all, so that a regulation instituted for the public good may be observed with willing obedience and due care. The prices for the sale of individual items which no one may exceed are listed below.

Diocletian, shown wearing a laurel wreath, a symbol of victory, initiated several important reforms.

This sculpture of the four Tetrarchs embracing one another rests outside St. Mark's Cathedral in Venice, Italy.

edict, issued in 301. We "hasten to apply the remedies long demanded by the [crippling economic] situation," he said,

satisfied that there can be no complaints. . . . With mankind itself now appearing to be praying for release [from financial problems], we have decreed that there be established . . . a maximum [ceiling for prices and wages], so that when the violence of high prices appears anywhere—may the gods avert such a calamity![28]

Although Diocletian's edict had the force of law behind it, this effort to cap prices failed. The exact reasons are not completely clear, but it appears that many people resented being told what they could earn or charge for goods. Whatever their motivations may have been, a majority of citizens either ignored the new price caps or found ways to get around them.

Diocletian's most sweeping reform was a reorganization of the Empire itself. He realized that administering so vast a realm was too difficult for one man, so he divided it in half. He himself took charge of the eastern sector, ruling from the city of Nicomedia (in northern Asia Minor); as emperor of the western sector, he appointed a general named Maximian. In 293 Diocletian further divided imperial power. He and Maximian each retained the title of Augustus, and each appointed an assistant emperor with the title of Caesar, creating a four-man combi-

choice but to continue to pay the army and its creditors with devalued coins. And prices remained abnormally high.

So Diocletian tried a more direct approach. He reasoned that regulating, or placing maximum caps on, prices and wages might stop the rise of inflation and make goods and services affordable to more people. He explained the theory behind his earnest but simpleminded plan in the introduction to his famous economic nation often referred to as "the Tetrarchy." Diocletian also reduced the size of many of the provinces and greatly enlarged their number, from about fifty provinces to one hundred.

The Last Persecution

Another important event of Diocletian's reign was Rome's last large-scale persecution of the Christians. Despite the ravages of prior persecutions, the Christians had persevered and their ranks had continued to grow, though very slowly. By the year 300 they made up roughly 5 percent of the Empire's population. Diocletian tolerated them at first, although he worried that their supposed crimes might anger the traditional gods. He finally decided to move against them in 303 following charges that

they had cast an evil spell that had tainted a traditional state religious ceremony. Diocletian's Caesar, Galerius, who had a particular hatred of Christians, convinced Diocletian to close the Christian churches. Soon, numerous Christian writings were burned, and many members of the sect were either killed or imprisoned.

For the most part, the persecution was confined to the eastern part of the Roman realm, the power base of Diocletian and Galerius. In the west, Maximian's Caesar, Constantius, who then controlled Gaul and Britain and enjoyed friendly contacts with Christian leaders there, showed the victims of the persecution mercy. He closed some churches, perhaps to make it look like he was following the party line, but took no further action. This humane policy helped

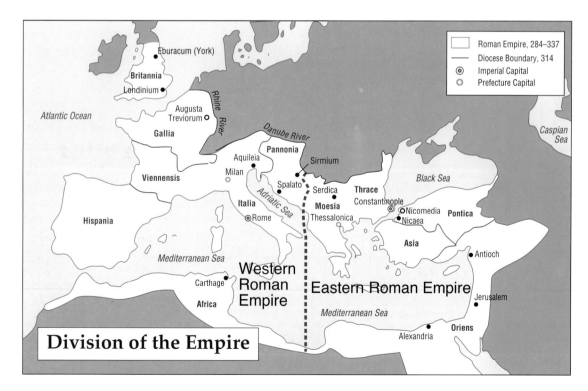

Division of the Empire

to blunt the overall effects of the anti-Christian crusade.

Also contributing to the ultimate failure of the persecution was a diversion of the government's attention and energies to pressing political and military events. In 305, tired of his strenuous duties as chief emperor, Diocletian became the Empire's first ruler to voluntarily give up the throne. Before abdicating, he formed a second tetrarchy, hoping its four partners would get along and maintain the peace. But to his dismay, the plan did not go as he had wished. In the next few years a power struggle erupted among the tetrarchs and some of their sons, and soon there was a full-blown civil war. Several different men proclaimed themselves emperor (or were proclaimed by their troops) while fighting major battles all over the Empire.

The Rise of Constantine

The climax of this round of conflict came in 312, when Constantius's son, Constantine, marched his army into Italy. His goal was to unseat one of the imperial claimants, Maxentius, who had illegally declared himself emperor and seized the city of Rome. Hoping to intercept and destroy the approaching enemy, Maxentius led his own troops out of the city via the Milvian Bridge.

Soon, however, Maxentius found his route blocked by Constantine's soldiers,

Constantine's soldiers, with shields bearing a Christian symbol (at far right) charge the enemy in the battle fought at the Milvian Bridge in 312.

whose shields bore a strange insignia—what looked like the letter *X* superimposed over a letter *I* with its top twisted into a loop. Maxentius did not realize that this insignia was a Christian symbol. Like his father, Constantine had long had friendly relations with Christians and was willing to accept their help in fighting his enemies. According to Constantine's contemporary biographer, the Christian bishop Eusebius, the day before, Constantine had been praying, when

> a most marvelous sign appeared to him from heaven. . . . He said that at about noon, when the day was already beginning to decline, he saw with his own eyes the trophy of a cross of light in the heavens, above the sun, and an inscription, CONQUER BY THIS, attached to it. At this sight he himself was struck with amazement, and his whole army also, which followed him on his expedition and witnessed the miracle.[29]

The truth of this account remains highly disputed. What seems more certain is that Constantine earnestly believed that the Christian god helped him win the day. Maxentius retreated back to the Milvian Bridge, where the two armies clashed and he and several thousand of his men died in a bloodbath. The next day, October 29, 312, Constantine entered Rome in triumph.

Constantine Boosts the Christian Cause

Constantine's victory and belief that the Christian god had played a key role in it explain the favor and support he showed the Christians in the years to come. Contrary to a popular misconception, he did not actually convert to the faith right away. For a long time he remained a pagan who accepted the existence of and showed favor and gratitude to the Christian god along with a number of traditional gods.

The first major expression of the gratitude Constantine felt he owed the Christians was official toleration for their faith. The pivotal decree became known as the Edict of Milan. It was named for a meeting held in that northern Italian city in February 313 between Constantine, now firmly in control of the western part of the realm, and Valerius Licinius, master of most of the eastern part. The Edict stated in part:

> [We] give both to Christians and to all others free facility to follow the religion which each may desire. All restrictions which were previously put forward in official pronouncements concerning the sect of the Christians should be removed, and . . . each one of them who freely and sincerely carries out the purpose of observing the Christian religion may endeavor to practice its precepts without any fear or danger.[30]

The good relations Constantine and Licinius established at Milan did not last long, however. The two rulers clashed in still another civil war and on July 3, 324, Constantine won an overwhelming victory. In the remaining thirteen years of his reign, he was the Empire's sole ruler.

During these years, Constantine continued to support the Christians and help

A painting executed for a Renaissance tapestry depicts Constantine overseeing the laying of the foundation stone of the city of Constantinople.

them gain acceptance in Roman society. He also played a chief role in church affairs as the mediator of several serious disputes that arose among the bishops, whom he recognized as the faith's political as well as spiritual leaders. Now that Christianity was considered a legitimate religion, it was only natural that he would assume such a role. By tradition, the Roman government, and in particular the emperor, had the duty of maintaining good relations between the Roman nation and the gods.

Constantine performed another important service for Christianity, as well as for the Empire itself, by establishing Constantinople, "the City of Constantine." His main initial reason was probably the perceived need to establish a strong base from which to defend the Empire's eastern sphere against attacks from the north and east. Its location on the Bosphorus Strait was a strategically strong position for the command and defense of Greece in the west, Asia Minor in the east, and the Black and Aegean seas.

However, because of the emperor's support for the Christians and their increasing power and influence, Constantinople also grew into a mighty Christian bastion. Indeed, at the inaugural festivities on May 11, 330, the emperor dedicated the city to the Virgin Mary and Holy Trinity. Constantine also poured vast sums of money into church-building programs, both in Constantinople and many other cities across the realm.

The final boost Constantine gave the Christian cause was an act he performed on his deathbed. Shortly before Easter in 337, he became seriously ill and, feeling that death was near, asked to be baptized. Available evidence suggests that by this time he was a committed Christian, and the fact that he received this sacrament so late in life does not mean that he still harbored doubts about the faith. At the time,

This Renaissance painting depicts Constantine's baptism, an event that provided a major boost for the long oppressed Christians.

baptism was considered a very serious step to take, and many people waited as long as possible to be baptized so that they would be less likely to commit a mortal sin before dying and meeting their maker.

Mounting Problems

While helping the Christians gain security, credibility, and influence, Constantine managed to keep the Empire intact and under the control of a single emperor. But as time went on, it became increasingly clear that Diocletian had been right; maintaining order and security in such a large realm was a superhuman task beyond the abilities of one person. In the second half of the fourth century, therefore, the division between the western and eastern Roman spheres continued and became more pronounced. Theodosius I, who died in 395, was the last emperor to rule both Roman spheres. (He did so only briefly; for most of his reign he ruled only eastern Rome.)

Even this division of authority did not solve the Empire's growing problems, many of which had persisted since the preceding century. The economy continued its downward slide, poverty remained rampant, and the building of new cities and public works (with the major exception of churches) almost ceased. Also, enemies continued to press on the borders, among them the Sassanians in the east.

It did not help that many of the Roman leaders charged with dealing with these

The Christians Strike Back

In the increasingly pro-Christian social and political climate of the late fourth century, Roman paganism came increasingly under attack. Some Christians vandalized or destroyed pagan statues, shrines, and temples across the realm, while zealous Christian priests denounced pagan beliefs and worship from the pulpit. The most influential of these clergymen was Ambrose of Milan (born ca. 340), a bishop who helped to complete the Christian revolution that Constantine had started. Ambrose showed no tolerance or respect for the religious views of others. He felt that his own faith was the only true one and that pagan beliefs must be suppressed and eradicated. To this end, he persuaded the western emperor Gratian (reigned 367–383) to relinquish his post as chief priest of the state religion, which all emperors since Augustus had held. Ambrose also convinced Gratian to take away government funding for the state priesthood and to remove the time-honored statue of the goddess Victory from the Roman Senate. Viewing the latter act as both intolerant and insensitive, leading pagans pleaded their case to the government. Ambrose's influence was too strong, however, and the statue was never returned to the Senate.

problems wasted precious time and energy fighting one another. For example, the dying Constantine had ordained that his sons—Constantine II, Constantius II, and Constans—should divide the imperial power equally after his death. But almost immediately a bloody power struggle erupted among the brothers. The ensuing civil strife did not end until 351, when Constantius II emerged the victor. He died in 361, and a distant relative, Julian, succeeded him. Julian was an unusually capable and humane ruler, but he perished in battle only two years into his reign, so his great potential was never realized.

Julian was also the last pagan Roman emperor. All of the rulers who succeeded him were devout Christians. Indeed, after Constantine's passing Christianity underwent nothing less than spectacular growth and in Theodosius's reign became the realm's official religion. But the Christian emperors and their officials were as unsuccessful in solving the Empire's many problems as their pagan predecessors. When Theodosius died near the close of the fourth century, Rome was in many ways actually worse off than it had been a century before. As has happened so often in history, the beginning of a new order ominously signaled the end of an old one. Christianity had triumphed, but Rome was doomed.

The emperor Theodosius (wearing the red cape) greets Ambrose, the most famous and influential Christian bishop of the late fourth century.

Chapter Seven

Eagle in the Dust: The Fall of Western Rome

R ome fell in the latter part of the fifth century. But the word *fall*, so often used to describe this momentous event, is often misunderstood. First, it was only the western portion of the Empire, encompassing Italy, north Africa, and western Europe, that ceased to exist. The eastern part of the realm, centered at Constantinople, endured until 1453.

Second, western Rome's fall was not a sudden event but rather a slow disintegration that encompassed several generations. Contributing to Rome's ultimate decline and fall were numerous internal problems. These included, among others, economic decay, civil wars, religious and political divisions between pagans and Christians, increasing administrative corruption, and social apathy.

However, these internal problems did not bring about Rome's end by themselves. Indeed, over time the Romans may well have solved them and survived, if it had not been for the intervention of larg-

er external events. Recent scholarship has come to see these domestic factors, at least individually speaking, more as part of Rome's continuing evolution than as agents of its doom. From this point of view, they were merely temporary setbacks in the Empire's struggle to reinvent itself after the setbacks of the third century.

The strongest evidence suggests that what ultimately did Rome in was a long series of pounding blows by invading barbarian tribes, coupled with an increasing inability of Roman armies to repel these intruders. The French historian André Piganiol aptly summed it up in the now famous phrase, "Roman civilization did not die a natural death. It was murdered."[31] Military historian Arther Ferrill concurs and adds that the Empire unwittingly contributed to its own demise by allowing its military to deteriorate in size and quality in its final century:

After [the year] 410, the emperor in the West could no longer project military power to the ancient frontiers. That weakness led immediately to the loss of Britain and within a generation to the loss of Africa. . . . The shrinkage of the imperial frontiers from 410 to 440 was directly the result of military conquests by barbarian forces . . . and Rome fell to the onrush of barbarism.[32]

The Advance of the Barbarians

Why did the barbarians attack Rome again? After defeating various northern tribes in the closing years of the third century, the Romans encountered only minimal troubles with them for several decades. But Germany, Scandinavia, and other regions lying north of the Empire were not static during these years. Local populations were rising and pressures to find new, fertile lands were building. What was needed was some dramatic event to set in motion folk migrations far larger than Europe had ever seen.

That fateful event occurred in the 370s. The Huns, a warlike nomadic people from central Asia, swept into eastern Europe, driving the Goths and other German tribes into the Roman border provinces. The fourth-century Roman historian Ammianus Marcellinus penned a graphic description of the Huns, calling them "abnormally savage." They had short,

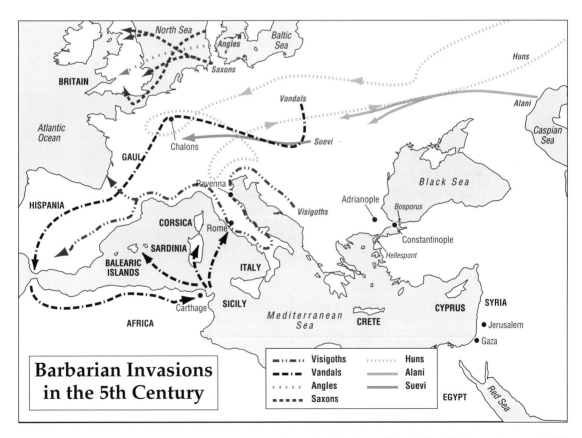

Barbarian Invasions in the 5th Century

Visigoths
Vandals
Angles
Saxons
Huns
Alani
Suevi

squat bodies and thick necks, he went on, and were

> so prodigiously ugly and bent that they might be two-legged animals. . . . Their way of life is so rough that they have no use for fire or seasoned food, but live on the roots of wild plants and the half-raw flesh of any sort of animals, which they warm a little by placing it between their thighs and the backs of their horses.[33]

In the wake of the advancing Huns, the Goths, Vandals, Burgundians, Franks, Angles, Alani, Saxons, and many other tribes spread over Europe in search of new lands. As many as two hundred thousand members of one branch of the Goths, the Visigoths (meaning "Wise Goths"), poured across the Danube into Rome's northeastern provinces. The eastern emperor, Valens, allowed these refugees to settle, perhaps hoping to recruit their warriors for his army.

However, the emperor's agents unwisely insulted and tried to exploit the Visigoths, who responded by pillaging their way through the province of Thrace. Valens hastened with an army to put down this

The Huns invade the territory of the Alani in eastern Europe. The Alani and other tribes menaced by the Huns then fled into Roman lands.

The Romans Adopt Barbarian Tactics

One clear sign that the Roman army was rapidly changing during the fourth and fifth centuries was the adoption of German-style formations and tactics by the Roman military. Perhaps the most common of the formations was the *cuneus,* which modern scholars used to think was shaped like a wedge or an arrowhead. The *cuneus* was more likely a square or rectangular attack column made up of a dense mass of men. Its width probably averaged twenty-five men and its depth sixteen, though this likely varied from one place and time to another. "Once the men in the column launched a charge," historian Simon Macdowall suggests in his *Late Roman Infantrymen,* "the neat alignment of the ranks and files would naturally be lost and the men in the center, feeling more secure, would surge forward, while those to the flanks [sides] might hang back." For this reason, the formation could quickly become disorganized and lose its cohesion.

uprising. But instead of waiting for reinforcements from his nephew, the western emperor Gratian, he imprudently attacked the much larger enemy force on his own near Adrianople, in eastern Thrace. On that dark day for Rome, August 9, 378, the overconfident Valens died along with two-thirds of his army, perhaps as many as forty thousand men.

This single defeat, though crippling, was not enough to bring down the Empire. Yet it marked a crucial turning point for Rome, the beginning of a military-political downward spiral that would eventually seal its fate. Moreover, an even more critical turn in barbarian-Roman affairs occurred soon afterward. Gratian appointed the respected army general Theodosius to succeed Valens. In 382 Theodosius negotiated a deal with the Visigoths, allowing them to settle in Thrace permanently. In return for providing troops for the Roman army, they were free from taxation and could serve under their own leaders, making them *foederati*, "federates," or equal allies living within the Empire. This set an ominous precedent for the future. As historian Charles Freeman puts it, "This was the first time that an area within the borders of the Empire had been passed out of effective Roman control."[34]

The Decline of the Army

As time went on, one barbarian tribe after another acquired federate status in the western provinces, a trend that steadily weakened the western Empire. On the one hand, the Roman government lost much of its authority over an increasing amount of territory. On the other, large numbers of warriors from these tribes joined the Roman army. Over time, this trend, which modern historians call the "barbarization" of the Roman army, negatively affected the discipline of the troops and their willingness to fight and die for Rome. Both of these qualities diminished over time, until finally they nearly disappeared, since by the 440s almost all of the men in the army were Germans rather than native Romans. According to Ferrill, as early as the 380s the German recruits immediately began to show

> an independence that in drill, discipline and organization meant catastrophe. They fought under their own native commanders, and the barbaric system of discipline was in no way as severe as the Roman. Eventually Roman soldiers saw no reason to do what barbarian troops in Roman service were rewarded heavily for not doing. . . . Too long and too close association with barbarian warriors, as allies in the Roman army, had ruined the qualities that made Roman armies great. . . . The Roman army of A.D. 440, in the west, had become little more than a barbarian army itself.[35]

In addition to the barbarization of the army, other factors contributed to the decline of Rome's military. As both the central government and local leaders increasingly encountered economic problems, for instance, the tasks and duties of the average Roman soldier became more and more thankless and hopeless. The soldiers not only received little pay, but their wages were also often months or even years in arrears, which severely damaged morale.

The problem of recruiting native Romans became still worse in the last two decades of the fourth century and on into the fifth, especially in the western portion of the realm. This was partly because the western provinces were less populous than the eastern ones. The increasingly widespread refusal of Christians to join and fight was also a contributing factor. In response, the government became desperate and not only recruited more and more barbarians but also passed laws designed to force native Romans into the army.

At the same time, some potential recruits resorted to extreme measures to dodge the draft, including cutting off their own thumbs. When this practice became widespread, the government at first ordered that such shirkers be burned alive. But later, as the authorities became more desperate, they let such self-mutilated individuals live and forced them to serve in the army despite their handicap. As these problems grew worse and took their toll over time, the traditional Roman soldier and army—highly disciplined, well organized, tough, eager, and willing to defend both family and the Roman state—steadily deteriorated.

The Sack of Rome

Other factors, which by themselves may not have been critical, made the effects of the barbarian invasions and decline of the army even worse. One of these was the permanent division of the Empire into western and eastern spheres. Before he died in 395, Theodosius arranged for his two young sons—Honorius and Arcadius —to rule in the west and east respective-

Alaric and his Visigoths enter Rome in 410. This was the first time the city's walls had been breached by a foreign foe in eight centuries.

ly. But this turn of events disturbed the Visigoths. In their minds, the deal they had earlier made with Theodosius might only be valid while he personally sat on the throne. Now that he was gone and his sons ruled separate sections of the realm, the Visigoths might lose their federate status and perhaps suffer in other ways.

In an effort to remain secure, the various Visigothic bands came together under one ruler—Alaric. He tried to renegotiate the treaty of 382 and also demanded that the central government give him com-

mand of a Roman army. The government turned him down. So he led his warriors on a rampage through Thrace. Over the course of the next few years Alaric continued making demands, and in 402 he marched his army on Italy.

The Romans managed to halt this advance, but they had only temporarily slowed the Visigoths. A few years later, Alaric marched on Rome again, capturing the city on August 24, 410. The invaders stayed only a few days and did little physical damage to the many stately public

The Vandals

The original homeland of the Vandals, one of the strongest of the barbarian tribes that threatened Rome, seems to have been northern Germany, near the Baltic Sea. By the mid-second century A.D., however, they had migrated southward to the region now occupied by Hungary. In the years to come, they periodically raided Roman border provinces. But they posed a much bigger threat beginning in the early fifth century when they joined other Germans in crossing the Rhine River into Gaul. Soon, feeling pressure from other barbarian groups entering Gaul, the Vandals moved farther south into Spain. Finally, in 429, they landed in Africa, swept eastward, overrunning the region's Roman provinces, and established a new and powerful Vandal kingdom, with its capital at Carthage. Not satisfied with these gains, in 455 the Vandals sailed north to Italy's western coast, sacked Rome, and also terrorized the coasts of Sicily, Sardinia, and Corsica. The Vandal kingdom survived the western Empire's fall (in 476) and prospered until the 530s, when an expedition sent by the eastern emperor Justinian destroyed it.

The Vandals loot Rome in 455. Ever since, their name has been synonymous with pillaging.

buildings. The real and more lasting injury was psychological in nature, for it was the first time that "invincible" Rome had been entered by a foreign foe in eight hundred years. The event sent shock waves through the whole Mediterranean world.

In this same period, other restless and ambitious tribes threatened the Empire's integrity. In 406, armies of Vandals, Alani, and Suevi invaded Gaul and some forged onward into Rome's Spanish provinces. Because Honorius's government lacked the money and men to stop them, the intruders were able to settle permanently in the conquered regions. Little by little, piece by piece, the western portion of the realm was captured and absorbed by barbarian tribes. And the emperors simply lacked the money, manpower, and military ingenuity to mount a counteroffensive on the huge scale that was needed.

The Last Western Emperor

Indeed, the quality of Rome's leadership continued to decline. The last nine western emperors were all weak rulers who lacked the talent and resources to protect the remaining Roman heartland. They were unable to stop a second sack of Rome in March 455. Led by a king named Gaiseric, the Vandals looted the city for two weeks. Three years later they further crippled and humiliated the Empire by capturing Sicily, which had been a cherished Roman possession for almost seven centuries.

By this time, in fact, there was little left in the western Empire that could be called Roman in the traditional sense. That once great realm now consisted of little more than the Italian peninsula and portions of a few nearby provinces. Moreover, most of the soldiers still defending these lands, including the generals, were of barbarian birth and had little understanding of or concern for the old Roman ideals and traditions.

On September 4, 476, the leading German-born general, Flavius Odoacer, led a contingent of troops into Ravenna, which by this time had replaced Rome as the western capital. He demanded that the current emperor, Romulus Augustulus, step down. Feeling that he had no other choice, the young man did so and quietly retired to Naples. Odoacer became king of Italy and thereafter no Roman emperors ruled in the west. For this reason, later historians came to mark Romulus Augustulus's forced abdication as the end of the traditional western imperial government and the "fall of Rome."

An Ancient Prophecy Fulfilled?

At the time, most Romans did not think their civilization was doomed. After all, Rome and other cities of the former Empire still stood; they simply had barbarian rulers rather than Roman ones. Perhaps, many people hoped, nonbarbarian leaders would eventually gain the upper hand and restore the integrity of western Rome.

Still, even the most optimistic observers recognized that the loss of most of the provinces and the ascendancy of barbarian rulers marked a major and dismal watershed in Rome's long history. And people naturally searched for someone or something to blame. Pagan Romans

In 476 Odoacer forces Romulus Augustulus to abdicate the throne, marking the official end of the western Roman Empire.

blamed the Christians, saying that the old gods had punished the Empire for accepting Christianity. Conversely, Christian Romans claimed that God had punished Rome for the sins of its pagan years.

Other people looked to ancient prophecy for an explanation. According to legend, before establishing Rome in 753 B.C. Romulus had seen twelve eagles flying together. The eagle became Rome's national symbol. But in the centuries that followed a superstition lingered, one that interpreted Romulus's eagles as predictors of how long Rome would exist. Each eagle represented a century of that existence as a nation. The time span from 753 B.C. to A.D. 476—a total of 1,229 years—eerily matched the 1,200 years of the prophecy, many people pointed out.

Whether they blamed divine wrath, ancient prophecy, or the barbarian onslaught itself for their predicament, the inhabitants of Rome and Italy in the late fifth century could not guess what the future would bring. In the generations that followed, Rome became largely depopulated. Its massive monuments fell increasingly into decay, a process accelerated by people's dismantling of them to use the stones in cruder structures. The decay of memory also played a role, as people forgot their heritage and no longer identified themselves as Romans. Beneath the feet of medieval Italians, the once mighty Roman eagle lay buried in the dust of ages, never to rise again.

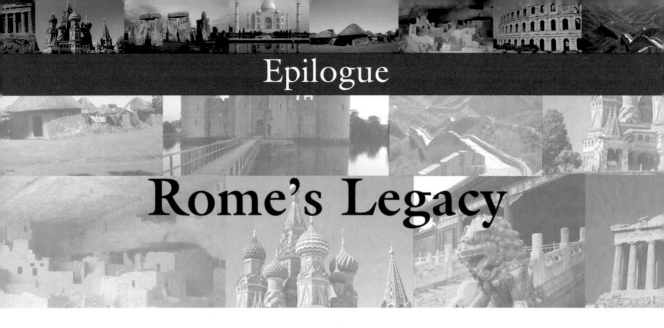

Epilogue

Rome's Legacy

After the fall of the western Roman Empire, the European-Mediterranean world underwent a gradual but steady transformation. The eastern part of the Roman realm survived the barbarian invasions and slowly mutated into what modern scholars call the Byzantine Empire. Centered at Constantinople, it used Greek, rather than Latin, as its official language. Also, Christian rituals there became distinct from those in the west, resulting in a religious split between the Eastern Orthodox Church in the east and the Roman Catholic Church in the west. After several centuries of vigorous life, the Byzantines (who still called themselves Romans) saw their own realm begin to shrink. And in 1453, its last remnants fell to the Ottoman Turks.

Meanwhile, in western Europe some of the small kingdoms established by the barbarians who had overrun Rome prospered. They became the many Italian, German, French, English, and Spanish realms of medieval times. (Also called the Middle Ages, this was the period beginning with western Rome's fall in 476 and ending in the 1500s.) Over time, these medieval kingdoms rose, fell, and combined in various ways to produce the major nations of modern Europe, which subsequently planted the seeds of other nations around the globe.

The Idea of Rome Lives On

In a very real sense, the spirit of ancient Rome remains alive in many of these lands. Though western Rome ceased to exist as a distinct political and social unit, its culture was far from dead and forgotten. Many of its cultural ideas and institutions survived in early medieval Europe and exerted an enormous impact on later European civilization and its offshoots. The modern Western world is therefore heavily indebted to the legacy of ancient Rome.

Among the more significant aspects of that legacy are elements of Roman law, language, and religion. European law courts adopted the concepts of trial by jury, impartial justice, and unwritten "laws of nature" from Roman law. And the Justinian Code, a massive sixth-century compilation of Roman statutes and commentaries on them, profoundly influenced later European justice systems.

No less influential was the means of expressing these laws. Adapted by diverse peoples, Latin gradually developed into the so-called Romance languages: French, Spanish, Portuguese, Italian, and Romanian; and the Germanic tongues of the Angles and Saxons mixed with Latin and French to form English, half the words of which are of Latin origin. Moreover, Latin survived as the leading language of European scholars as well as the official language of the Roman Catholic Church. As the ancient world transformed into the medieval, that church, which had risen to dominate Rome in its final two centuries, became the chief unifying force of European civilization, influencing and shaping daily life and thought.

To these profound legacies can be added many other modern institutions and concepts originated by the Romans (or adopted by them from the Greeks and others). A mere partial list includes postal systems, fire departments, central heating, glass windows, apartment buildings, sewer systems, social welfare benefits, and public education. In these and other ways, some essential elements of ancient Rome live on and will likely continue do so for a long time to come. One modern scholar puts it this way: "Rome never fell, [but simply] turned into something else. [When it ceased to be a] political power, [it] passed into even greater supremacy as an idea. Rome, with the Latin language, had become immortal."[36]

The ruins of Rome's Forum Romanum bear mute testimony to the power and grandeur of the society that built it.

Notes

Introduction: The Evidence from the Ashes

1. Pliny the Younger, *Letters*, in *The Letters of the Younger Pliny*, trans. Betty Radice. New York: Penguin, 1969, pp. 167–68.
2. Michael Grant, *Cities of Vesuvius: Pompeii and Herculaneum*. London: Phoenix, 2001, p. vii.

Chapter 1: From Republic to Empire: The Augustan Age

3. Quoted in Suetonius, *Lives of the Twelve Caesars*, published as *The Twelve Caesars*, trans. Robert Graves, rev. Michael Grant. New York: Penguin, 1979, p. 69.
4. Tacitus, *Annals*, published as *Tacitus: The Annals of Imperial Rome*, trans. Michael Grant. New York: Penguin, 1989, p. 32.
5. Augustus, *Res gestae*, in *Sources in Western Civilization: Rome*, ed. William G. Sinnegin. New York: Free, 1965, p. 109.

Chapter 2: Rome of the Caesars: The First Century of Peace

6. Tacitus, *Annals*, p. 157.
7. Quoted in Suetonius, *Twelve Caesars*, p. 168.
8. Quoted in Suetonius, *Twelve Caesars*, p. 170.

9. Suetonius, *Twelve Caesars*, p. 228.
10. Tacitus, *Annals*, p. 365.
11. Suetonius, *Twelve Caesars*, p. 243.
12. Suetonius, *Twelve Caesars*, p. 285.
13. Suetonius, *Twelve Caesars*, p. 295.

Chapter 3: Bread and Circuses: Attempts to Maintain Control

14. Juvenal, *Satires*, published as *Juvenal: The Sixteen Satires*, trans. Peter Green. New York: Penguin, 1974, p. 207.
15. Quoted in Jo-Ann Shelton, ed. and trans., *As the Romans Did: A Sourcebook in Roman Social History*. New York: Oxford University Press, 1997, p. 336.
16. Pliny the Younger, *Letters*, p. 236.

Chapter 4: The Five Good Emperors: Rome at Its Zenith

17. Edward Gibbon, *The Decline and Fall of the Roman Empire*, vol. 1, ed. David Womersley. New York: Penguin, 1994, pp. 101, 103.
18. Quoted in Pliny the Younger, *Letters*, pp. 293, 295.
19. *Augustan History*, published as *Lives of the Later Caesars, the First Part of the Augustan History, with Newly Compiled Lives of Nerva and Trajan*, trans. Anthony Birley. New York: Penguin, 1976, p. 77.
20. Marcus Aurelius, *Meditations*, trans. George Long, in *Lucretius, Epictetus, Marcus Aurelius*. Chicago: Encyclopaedia Britannica, 1952, pp. 254–55.

21. Aelius Aristides, *Roman Panegyric*, quoted in Naphtali Lewis and Meyer Reinhold, eds., *Roman Civilization, Sourcebook II: The Empire*. New York: Harper and Row, 1966, pp. 137–38.
22. Marcus Aurelius, *Meditations*, p. 276.

Chapter 5: The Anarchy: Rome on the Brink of Collapse

23. *Augustan History*, pp. 163, 165–66.
24. Quoted in Dio Cassius, *Roman History*, published as *Dio's History of Rome and Annals of the Roman People*, trans. Herbert B. Foster. Troy, NY: Pafraets, 1906, p. 387.
25. Quoted in Lewis and Reinhold, *Roman Civilization, Sourcebook II*, pp. 437–38.
26. A.H.M. Jones, *Constantine and the Conversion of Europe*. Toronto, Canada: University of Toronto Press, 1979, pp. 19–21.
27. Michael Grant, *The Fall of the Roman Empire*. New York: Macmillan, 1990, p. 3.

Chapter 6: Rule by Sword and Cross: The Later Empire

28. Diocletian, *Economic Edict*, quoted in Lewis and Reinhold, *Roman Civilization, Sourcebook II*, p. 463.
29. Eusebius, *Life of Constantine*, excerpts translated in *Caesars and Saints: The Rise of the Christian State, A.D. 180–313*, by Stewart Perowne. New York: Barnes and Noble, 1992, p. 175.
30. Constantine and Licinius, *Edict of Milan*, quoted in *The Middle Ages*, vol. 1. *Sources of Medieval History*, ed. Brian Tierney. New York: Knopf, 1973, pp. 20–21.

Chapter 7: Eagle in the Dust: The Fall of Western Rome

31. André Piganiol, "The Causes of the Ruin of the Roman Empire," in *The End of the Roman Empire: Decline or Transformation?* ed. Donald Kagan. Boston: D.C. Heath, 1992, p. 91.
32. Arther Ferrill, *The Fall of the Roman Empire: The Military Explanation*. New York: Thames and Hudson, 1988, pp. 164–69.
33. Ammianus Marcellinus, *History*, published as *The Later Roman Empire, A.D. 354–378*, trans. and ed. Walter Hamilton. New York: Penguin, 1986, pp. 411–12.
34. Charles Freeman, *Egypt, Greece, and Rome: Civilizations of the Ancient Mediterranean*. Oxford, England: Oxford University Press, 2004, p. 507.
35. Ferrill, *Fall of the Roman Empire*, pp. 84–85, 140.

Epilogue: Rome's Legacy

36. R.H. Barrow, *The Romans*. Baltimore: Penguin, 1990, p. 204.

For Further Reading

Books

Lionel Casson, *Everyday Life in Ancient Rome.* Baltimore: Johns Hopkins University Press, 2001. A well-written presentation by a highly respected scholar of how the Romans lived: their homes, streets, entertainments, eating habits, theaters, religion, slaves, marriage customs, tombstone epitaphs, and more.

Peter Connolly, *Pompeii.* New York: Oxford University Press, 1994. Beautifully illustrated by Connolly himself, this is a splendid look at the famous buried city and what scholars have learned from it.

Susie Hodge, *Roman Art.* Crystal Lake, IL: Heineman Library, 1998. A short but well-illustrated and informative look at ancient Roman art and sculpture.

John Malam, *Secret Worlds: Gladiators.* London: Dorling Kindersley, 2002. A beautifully illustrated book that brings the exciting but bloody gladiatorial combats of ancient Rome to life.

Geraldine McCaughrean, *Roman Myths.* New York: Margaret McElderry, 2001. A well-written, enthusiastic introduction to Roman mythology for young people.

Don Nardo, *The Age of Augustus.* San Diego: Lucent, 1996. An overview of the reign and accomplishments of the man who created the Roman Empire and oversaw the golden age of Roman literature.

———, *Roman Amphitheaters.* New York: Franklin Watts, 2002. Tells about the origins of the stone arenas where gladiators and animal hunters fought and often died, how these structures were built, and the variety of games they showcased.

Web Sites

A Day at the Baths, PBS Secrets of Lost Empires (www.pbs.org/wgbh/nova/lostempires/roman/day.html). A virtual tour of a large Roman bathhouse, including recent photos of excavated sections of these structures.

Ludus Gladiatorius, English Reenactor Group (www.ludus.org.uk). The main page has many links that take the reader on a fascinating journey into modern attempts to restage ancient Roman gladiatorial bouts with authentic costumes, weapons, and tactics.

Roman Dress, Illustrated History of the Roman Empire (www.roman-empire.net/society/soc-dress.html). A very informative site about everyday Roman clothing, supplemented by photos and drawings.

Women in Roman Society, Discovery Channel (http://myron.sjsu.edu/romeweb/LADYCONT/LADY CONT.htm). This site provides a long list of links, each leading to a biography of a noted Roman woman.

Works Consulted

Major Works

J.P.V.D. Balsdon, *Life and Leisure in Ancient Rome.* London: Phoenix, 2002. This huge, detailed, and masterful volume by a highly respected historian is one of the best general studies of Roman life, customs, and traditions.

Anthony A. Barrett, *Agrippina: Sex, Power, and Politics in the Early Empire.* New Haven, CT: Yale University Press, 1996. An impressive study of Nero's mother and her influence on the imperial court and government.

Averil Cameron, *The Later Roman Empire: A.D. 284–430.* Cambridge, MA: Harvard University Press, 1993. A well-written, somewhat scholarly study of Diocletian's and Constantine's administrative and other reforms.

Arther Ferrill, *The Fall of the Roman Empire: The Military Explanation.* New York: Thames and Hudson, 1988. Ferrill builds a strong case for the idea that Rome fell mainly because its army grew increasingly less disciplined and formidable during the Empire's last two centuries.

John B. Firth, *Augustus Caesar and the Organization of the Empire of Rome.* Manchester, NH: Ayer, 2002. A detailed, thoughtful telling of the final years of the Republic and his ascendancy as Augustus, the first Roman emperor.

Michael Grant, *The Antonines: The Roman Empire in Transition.* London: Routledge, 1996. A penetrating, informative look at Antoninus Pius, Marcus Aurelius, Lucius Verus, and Commodus—and how they ruled the Empire

———, *Constantine the Great: The Man and His Times.* New York: Scribner's, 1994. An excellent study of Constantine, his achievements (Christianity, Constantinople, etc.), and his impact on the Roman Empire and later ages.

———, *The Fall of the Roman Empire.* New York: Macmillan, 1990. Grant outlines the many manifestations of disunity (the generals turning on the state, the poor versus the rich, etc.) that caused the Empire's decline.

———, *History of Rome.* London: Orion, 1996. Comprehensive, insightful, and well written, this is one of the best available general overviews of Roman civilization.

Richard Holland, *Nero: The Man Behind the Myth.* Gloucestershire, England: Sutton, 2000. A fine recent piece of scholarship that shows Nero as a more complex and interesting character than he is usually portrayed.

A.H.M. Jones, *Constantine and the Conversion of Europe.* Toronto, Canada: University of Toronto Press, 1979. A superior general overview of Constantine's world and his influence, by one of the twentieth century's greatest Roman scholars.

———, *The Decline of the Ancient World.* London: Longman Group, 1966. *Note:* This is a shortened version of Jones's massive and highly influential *The Later Roman Empire, 284–602.* 3 vols. Baltimore: Johns Hopkins University Press, 1986 (originally 1964). An exhaustively detailed, endlessly informative work that touches on virtually every aspect of the history and culture of the Later Empire.

Eckart Kohne, ed., *Gladiators and Caesars: The Power of Spectacle in Ancient Rome.* Berkeley and Los Angeles: University of California Press, 2000. An in-depth, insightful, very well-written treatment of the subject.

Ramsay MacMullen, *Christianizing the Roman Empire,* A.D. *100–400.* New Haven, CT: Yale University Press, 1986. A superb examination of the rise of the Christians in the Roman Empire.

Chris Scarre, *Chronicle of the Roman Emperors.* New York: Thames and Hudson, 1995. A well-written general overview of the emperors, supplemented by numerous primary source material and useful timelines.

Pat Southern and Karen R. Dixon, *The Late Roman Army.* New Haven, CT: Yale University Press, 1996. This well-written, scholarly volume examines the gradual, nearly three-century-long decline of the Roman army and how its disintegration helped to spell Rome's doom.

Other Important Works

Primary Sources

Ammianus Marcellinus, *History,* published as *The Later Roman Empire,* A.D. *354–378.* Trans. and ed. Walter Hamilton. New York: Penguin, 1986.

Augustan History, published as *Lives of the Later Caesars, the First Part of the Augustan History, with Newly Compiled* Lives *of Nerva and Trajan.* Trans. Anthony Birley. New York: Penguin, 1976.

Leon Bernard and Theodore B. Hodges, eds., *Readings in European History.* New York: Macmillan, 1958.

Dio Cassius, *Roman History,* published as *Dio's History of Rome and Annals of the Roman People.* Trans. Herbert B. Foster. Troy, NY: Pafraets, 1906.

Juvenal, *Satires,* published as *Juvenal: The Sixteen Satires.* Trans. Peter Green. New York: Penguin, 1974.

Bernard Knox, ed., *The Norton Book of Classical Literature.* New York: W.W. Norton, 1993.

Naphtali Lewis and Meyer Reinhold, eds., *Roman Civilization, Sourcebook II: The Empire.* New York: Harper and Row, 1966.

Marcus Aurelius, *Meditations,* trans. George Long, in *Lucretius, Epictetus, Marcus Aurelius.* Chicago: Encyclopaedia Britannica, 1952.

Pliny the Younger, *Letters,* published as *The Letters of the Younger Pliny.* Trans. Betty Radice. New York: Penguin, 1969.

Jo-Ann Shelton, ed. and trans., *As the Romans Did: A Sourcebook in Roman Social History.* New York: Oxford University Press, 1997.

William G. Sinnegin, ed., *Sources in Western Civilization: Rome.* New York: Free, 1965.

Suetonius, *Lives of the Twelve Caesars,* published as *The Twelve Caesars.* Trans.

Robert Graves. Rev. Michael Grant. New York: Penguin, 1979.

Tacitus, *Annals*, published as *Tacitus: The Annals of Imperial Rome.* Trans. Michael Grant. New York: Penguin, 1989.

Brian Tierney, ed., *The Middle Ages.* Vol. 1. *Sources of Medieval History.* New York: Knopf, 1973.

Modern Sources

Lesley Adkins and Roy A. Adkins, *Handbook to Life in Ancient Rome.* New York: Facts On File, 2004.

R.H. Barrow, *The Romans.* Baltimore: Penguin, 1990.

John Boardman et al., *The Oxford History of the Roman World.* New York: Oxford University Press, 2001.

Lionel Casson, *Travel in the Ancient World.* Baltimore: Johns Hopkins University Press, 1994.

Peter Connolly, *Greece and Rome at War.* London: Green Hill, 1998.

Charles Freeman, *Egypt, Greece, and Rome: Civilizations of the Ancient Mediterranean.* Oxford, England: Oxford University Press, 2004.

Edward Gibbon, *The Decline and Fall of the Roman Empire*, ed. David Womersley. 3 vols. New York: Penguin, 1994.

Justo L. Gonzalez, *The Story of Christianity.* Vol. 1. *The Early Church to the Dawn of the Reformation.* San Francisco: Harper and Row, 1985.

Michael Grant, *Cities of Vesuvius: Pompeii and Herculaneum.* London: Phoenix, 2001.

———, *The Roman Emperors.* New York: Barnes and Noble, 1997.

———, *A Social History of Greece and Rome.* New York: Charles Scribner's Sons, 1992.

———, *The World of Rome.* London: Phoenix, 2000.

Peter Heather, *The Goths.* Cambridge, MA: Blackwell, 1996.

Harold W. Johnston, *The Private Life of the Romans.* Stockton, CA: University of the Pacific Press, 2002.

Donald Kagan, ed., *The End of the Roman Empire: Decline or Transformation?* Boston: D.C. Heath, 1992.

Robert B. Kebric, *Roman People.* New York: McGraw-Hill, Mayfield, 2005.

Lawrence Keppie, *The Making of the Roman Army.* New York: Barnes and Noble, 1998.

Simon Macdowall, *Late Roman Infantrymen, 236–565 A.D.* London: Osprey, 1994.

Stewart Perowne, *Caesars and Saints: The Rise of the Christian State, A.D. 180–313.* New York: Barnes and Noble, 1992.

Chris Scarre, *Historical Atlas of Ancient Rome.* New York: Penguin Books, 1995.

Chester G. Starr, *Civilization and the Caesars: The Intellectual Revolution in the Roman Empire.* New York: Norton, 1965.

———, *A History of the Ancient World.* New York: Oxford University Press, 1991.

Index

Picture Credits

Classical historian Don Nardo has published many volumes about ancient Roman history and culture, including *The Punic Wars, The Age of Augustus, A Travel Guide to Ancient Rome, Life of a Roman Gladiator, Greek and Roman Science,* and Greenhaven Press's massive *Encyclopedia of Greek and Roman Mythology.* Mr. Nardo also writes screenplays and teleplays and composes music. He lives in Massachusetts with his wife, Christine.